Forgotten Fields
of America

VOLUME TWO

World War II Bases and Training, then and now.

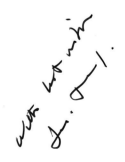

PICTORIAL HISTORIES PUBLISHING COMPANY, INC.
713 South Third Street West, Missoula, Montana 59801

Contents

Title page photo: Lt. P.J. McLaughlin (in front of and leaning against the tire of his B-29) at Pyote Army Air Field.

Acknowledgments

PROBABLY NO ONE writes a book by themselves and this is certainly true for me. I owe a deep debt of gratitude to my wife, Jane, who gave ideas, timely critiques, and encouragement. My daughter Elizabeth scoured the manuscript, put it into readable form, and accompanied me to one of the former training fields. My older son, David, flew me to three of the fields and with his help I was able to get some fine aerial views of the fields as they are today. My other son, Chip, visited some of the fields with me, helped me find my way about, and patiently endured my rambling. I feel gifted to have such a wonderful wife and three splendid children.

I met a lot of fine people while researching this book and I treasure their friendship. For me, meeting such people is a major benefit of my writing. Lots of people helped me in a number of ways, including answering questions, going out of their way to help, and sharing photos and memories. Many have become dear friends. My thanks to Rick Alter, Dave Bellmore, Earl Belt, Bill Berger, Reuben Bishop, Isabelle Blanchard, Otis Burrell, Suzanne Campbell, John Carah, Otha Carneal, Jim Carr, Joseph Caver, Floyd Clark, John Copeland, Lex Cralley, Joe Dickman, Archie Difante, Horace Dimond, Donald Doggett, Ed Doram, Louis Drake, Virgil Eiland, Bill Flippo, Buddy Frazier, Dorotha Giannangelo, Lillian Gondek, Quenten Hannawald, Howard Harrett, Warren Hasse, Evelyn Herrmann, Ernie Hix, Pat Hughen, Glenda Jones, Harlin Jones, Ted Jordan, Fritz Kahl, Donald Klinko, Harry Knight, Leroy Knorr, Tony Kretten, Linda Kuester, John Leahr, Jane Lempke, Roosevelt Lewis, Lea Lindeman, Rusty Lindeman, Jimmy Marks, Jean Martin, Mac McCallum, Robert McGuire, Bill McKee, P.J. McLaughlin, Ross McSwain, Howard Melton, Chris Melville, Dave Menard, Ed Miller, Godfrey Miller, Roger Myers, Bud Nelson, Lyle Nelson, Bill Ney Jr., Murl Nichols, George Ola, Ruth Ola, Silvo Pettinelli, Harry Ponder, Elmo Pope, Jimmy Porter, Lynn Post, Conrad Powell, Essie Roberts, Mildred Santiago, Bob Schultz, Melvin Scott, Earl Siddens, Jeanne Spraque, Bob Stoltz, Denny Swanstrom, George Swift, Bill Switzer, Edwin Sykes, Jack Taylor, Dallas Tohill, Maurey Topf, Christine Trebellas, Terry Turner, Chester Waldrup, Ray White, H. E. Williams, Johnny Williams, Roberta Williams, and Gerald Yagen.

I also want to remember three of my friends Horace Dimond, George Ola and Ed Shenk who passed away as the book was being written. I miss them. Finally, I want to express my appreciation and thanks to those who served their country and asked for nothing in return. When it counted, they were there, and it is because of their sacrifice that we enjoy the freedom we have today.

Introduction

I WROTE THIS BOOK, and the one that preceded it, to tell the story of one of the most magnificent and monumental events in the history of the United States. Largely forgotten today, it is the story of the build up of the United States Air Force just prior to and during World War II. It is also the story of the courage and self sacrifice of thousands of people who had their lives interrupted, and gave freely of themselves at a time when their country needed them.

From the poorly armed and understaffed Air Corps that existed at the time the first bombs were dropped on Pearl Harbor, the United States produced, just a few years later, the greatest Air Force the world has ever seen. The effort to achieve this was unprecedented. Thousands of fine young men gave their lives in training accidents. Often families who had lived on their land for generations were forced to move with little notice, their homes and buildings sold off or bulldozed into the ground so construction could begin. Within six months a small city replaced the farm or vacant land and training would start.

During the relatively short period from 1939 to late 1943 the Army Air Corps, later renamed the Army Air Forces, grew from just 17 air bases to 345 main bases, 116 subbases and 322 auxiliary fields. In addition, there were almost 500 bombing and gunnery ranges.

The training fields were small self contained towns that differed according to their use, but in many ways were the same. They varied in size from about 2000 acres for a basic flight training base to more than 65,000 acres for a base used to teach gunnery. The largest training field was Wendover Field with about 700 buildings and 3,500,000 acres. Thousands of men and women lived and worked on the bases either as trainers, trainees, support personnel, or family members. Typically the bases were built from scratch on farm or vacant land and contained several hun-dred buildings of all descriptions. Most fields had hangars, barracks, warehouses, hospitals, dental clinics, dining halls, and maintenance shops. There were libraries, social clubs for officers, and enlisted men, and stores to buy living necessities. Some training fields had swimming pools, all had sport fields. The facilities vital to the training mission were constructed first and that part took about six months. As time permitted, the "luxuries," i.e., swimming pools, libraries, and officers clubs were built as time and material permitted. Throughout the war, they were constantly improved to make living more comfortable and the training more efficient. Construction was of wood, tar paper, and non-masonry siding. The use of concrete and steel was limited because of the critical need elsewhere. Most buildings were hot and dusty in the summer and very cold in the winter.

It is still possible to find remnants of these training fields scattered across the United States. Many have been converted into municipal airports, some are industrial parks, and others remain as Air Force installations. Hundreds of the temporary buildings that were used at the training bases survive today, and are being used for other purposes. Occasionally, they are derelict, and it is possible to wander through them and see reminders of the activity that is now being lost in the backwaters of time.

This book tells the story of twelve of those fields and shows them as they were during World War II and at the time of the author's visit. Each of the fields has a fascinating history. To research the story, the author poured over thousands of frames of micro film, worked with historical societies, read newspaper accounts, and spoke with people who served at the fields. Their experiences helped to bring the fields to life and give the reader a glimpse of what happened at these training bases so long ago.

Aerial view of Freeman Field circa 1946. By this time, flying training had stopped and the field was being used by the Air Technical Command to store and evaluate captured enemy material.   (USAF)

Aerial view of Freeman Field as it is today. Notice the large parking ramp which once held the AT 10's used to train cadets in advanced twin engine flying. Two of the field's four runways are still in use for general aviation aircraft.   (LIZ)

1

The Luftwaffe in Indiana

FREEMAN FIELD—SEYMOUR, INDIANA

The finding in late 1997 of large quantities of Luftwaffe aircraft parts and other equipment at Freeman Field, Indiana was a significant aviation archaeological event. While it answers many questions about the role of Freeman Field at war's end, it only deepens and adds to the mystery of other rumors about this field's activities. One of the more important questions—what else may be buried here?

The story of German aircraft parts and their discovery at Freeman Field goes back to the closing days of WW II, and the field's role in the testing of captured Luftwaffe equipment. Early in the war, Freeman Field was an advanced twin engine training field, one of the hundreds used to train aircrew personnel during the war. The field is on the outskirts of Seymour Indiana about sixty miles south of Indianapolis; it was named to honor Captain Richard S. Freeman, a 1930 graduate of West Point. Captain Freeman helped establish Ladd Field—today's Wainwright Army Base—just outside Fairbanks, Alaska. He was Ladd Field's first commander. Captain Freeman held the Distinguished Flying Cross, was awarded the Mackay trophy, and was one of the pioneers of the Army Air Mail Service. He was killed on February 6, 1941, in the crash of a B-17 he was flying near Lovelock, Nevada. The aircraft was equipped

with the then secret Norden bombsight, and had extensive equipment for cold weather flying. The B-17 was on its way to Wright Field when it exploded in midair. Sabotage was suspected, but never proven. Captain Freeman grew up in Winamac, Indiana, where he graduated from Winamac High School, he died at age 33, and is buried in Winamac, Indiana.

Freeman Field was built on 2,653 acres of flat to rolling farm land, and had at its peak four runways, each 5500 feet long, and a total of 413 buildings. Today, the field is about the same size, with much of it leased to farmers who grow corn and soy beans. The runways are still here; however, two have been shut down. Most of the former cantonment area is now a thriving industrial park. There are about twelve buildings remaining from WWII. Also located on the field is a small, but growing museum that honors the field's contributions during WWII. The museum was started by the current airport manager, Mr. Ted Jordan, and is located in two of the former WWII buildings.

As mentioned, Freeman Field was a twin-engine advanced training school. The trainer used at Freeman was the Beechcraft AT-10 "Wichita." It was unique in that its construction was almost entirely of wood. At one time, there were about 200 of these aircraft assigned

General view of the dig site where the Luftwaffe parts were recovered. This site is near the old base incinerator and close to the former sub-depot. The sub-depot building still stands today and is used as a receiving and distribution facility. Since this photo was taken, additional buildings have been constructed on the site. (DIMOND)

for training purposes at the field. Today, none exist in flyable condition, probably because of the wood construction. There is, however, a magnificently restored example located at the United States Air Force Museum in Dayton, Ohio. More than 4000 pilots earned their wings flying this plane while at Freeman Field.

Freeman Field was the site for the USAAF first helicopter training school, established in September 1944. The helicopters were the Sikorsky R-4B, and were flown directly from the Sikorsky plant in Bridgeport, Connecticut. This was quite a daring trip for that time, one which set several records. Then, helicopters were so new and revolutionary that many people did not know what to call them. Outside of aviation circles, few had ever seen one. Some referred to them as a "direct lift" airplane. Also, efforts were made to insure that the word "helicopter" was pronounced correctly. Preparations for the arrival of the helicopters at Freeman Field were kept under a strict lid of secrecy. The group assigned to insure their smooth arrival was known as "Section B-O," and over time, the group became known as the "Lifebouy Kids." This was due to the then popular advertising phrase "B-O" (which stood for body odor) used by a well known deodorant soap named, Lifebouy. The helicopter program only lasted till December, when it was transferred to Chanute Field, at Rantoul, Illinois.

Freeman Field's unique story begins while the war in Europe was nearing its end. Training at the field had

An Arado Ar 234 at Freeman Field. Much of the Field's captured equipment was on display for the public in September 1945. The Arado Ar 234 was a highly advanced twin jet bomber/reconnaissance plane that came into use in 1944. (WHITE)

4

A V-2 rocket, flanked by a V-1 on either side, circa 1945, during a public display of the field's aircraft and other captured material. The two round objects near the V-2's base were probably fuel tanks for the V-2 rocket. (WHITE)

stopped, and it became the site for the storage of American and foreign aircraft. Most of the foreign airplanes were German, but there were also Japanese, Italian, and English planes. Nowhere in the United States would there be such large numbers of foreign aircraft, many of which were rare and incredibly advanced for their time. They included everything from high performance piston engine fighters, such as Me-109's and FW 190's, to exotic jets like the Me 262, He 162, Ar 234's and even V-1 and V-2 rockets. There were at least twenty five-different German aircraft at Freeman Field. In addition, over time, there would be warehouses full of Luftwaffe equipment such as fire control systems, parachutes, life rafts, field glasses, and much more. The equipment was here as a result of a directive from the Commanding General of the Army Air Forces, H. H. Arnold, that an airfield be found to be used as a repository and testing center for "enemy aeronautical equipment." In addition, the General wanted all significant U.S. aircraft to be temporarily stored here for an Army Air Forces museum, the site to

be determined at a later date. At this time, June 1945, Freeman Field was placed under the direct command of the Air Technical Service Command. The new mission of the field stated: " Freeman Field was established with the mission of receiving, reconditioning, evaluating, and storing at least one each of every item of enemy aircraft material. This was to include items such as clothing and parachutes as well as the aircraft themselves. Also, to be included were such items as anti aircraft guns, radar, and similar devices. The field will also assemble and catalogue U.S. equipment for display at the present and for the future A.A.F. museum, the site to be determined at a later date."

In charge of the Flight Maintenance Branch at Freeman Field was Captain H. Ray White. Captain White was an outstanding pilot and considered to be one of the best instrument pilots at Wright Field. Ray flew the first foreign aircraft to Freeman Field, a Junkers Ju 88. Often his skilled feel for an airplane was required to save himself and the plane when problems developed during flight testing of a reassembled

Captain White standing next to his favorite plane, the Bf-108. This was rumored to be Herman Goering's personal aircraft. It arrived at Freeman Field in crates painted in the gaudy orange and yellow colors. (WHITE)

aircraft. Ray remembers his first flight with the plane that would later become his favorite. It was almost his last. The aircraft, a Bf-108, was a five- place, low wing monoplane, painted red and orange, and rumored to have been the personal plane of Herman Goering, head of the Luftwaffe. The airplane had been reassembled at Freeman Field; however, on the initial flight, following reassembly, the cowl blew off while

Ray was in the middle of his takeoff run. Ray braked to a stop, taxied back down the runway, picked up the cowling, and returned to the engineering hangar. After the cowling was properly put on the plane, Ray took off again. This time, the ailerons locked immediately after take off. He called the tower, reported the problem, and explained that he would make a wide sweeping turn to line up with the runway. While approach-

A Heinkel He-162 A Salamander on display at Freeman Field. This aircraft was an attempt by the Luftwaffe to build a simple, easy to fly fighter. About 120 were produced but were too late to have any impact on the aerial war. (WHITE)

ing the runway, he lowered the wheels, and immediately regained aileron control. After checking, he found that the hydraulic lines were installed on the wrong side of the landing gear strut, a condition that bound the aileron cables after the gear was retracted. Later, Ray was ordered to return the plane to Wright Field, which he did reluctantly; however, he did not tell anyone the starting procedure. The ignition switch was a knot at the end of a cable which had to be pulled to turn on the ignition.

Some of the first flyable examples of German aircraft arrived at Freeman Field on the British aircraft carrier *HMS Reaper* when the ship docked at the port of Newark in late July 1945. Additional equipment such as engines, wings and fuselages, also arrived on the carrier and were shipped to Freeman Field by rail. Additional material was transported on a Liberty ship named the *Richard J. Gatling,* and perhaps other ships. After the arrival of planes and equipment at Freeman Field, the evaluation program swung into high gear. By necessity, the evaluation was on a broad scale basis and specific work was done at Wright Field, and in some cases, Muroc Dry Lake (Edwards Air Force Base). The early estimate of 75 officers and 705 enlisted men/ civilians to help conduct the evaluations was never reached. There were several reasons for this, but principally, with the war in Europe over and the swift conclusion to the war with Japan, there was no longer the critical need to find out what secrets the Germans had shared with the Japanese. Also, it was difficult to hire quality civilian help because the job was short term, severe housing problems existed, and the civilian personnel budget was

The author, on right, holding a piece of metal detection equipment used to locate favorable areas for further exploration. (OSBORN)

cut. Many key projects were set aside and never completed. Despite these drawbacks, considerable flying was done. For the first six months of operation, there were approximately 1,800 flights, both local and cross country, using foreign and U.S. aircraft. At one time, there were 71 American aircraft at the field. Shortly after the victory over Japan, Freeman Field's primary mission was changed. Less emphasis was placed on evaluation, and more upon the display of the aircraft and equipment at various exhibits and air shows across the country.

Over the next several months, activities at the field were shut down and efforts were made to dispose of the surplus equipment. Most of the aircraft were transferred to Davis Monthan Air Force Base, Wright Field, or the Douglas Plant in Chicago. Some gliders were towed by air to Orchard Place Airport (today's O'Hare Field). It appears that not all the planes assigned to Freeman Field were transferred. Some may have been left at the field and their final disposition is unknown. In addition to the aircraft, there was the captured Luftwaffe equipment and the usual material found at most airfields at their closing. Prior to the field's closing in 1947, considerable effort was made to dispose of some surplus material. Sales were held at the field; "Scrap Lumber to be Sold at Field for $2 per pick-up truckload" announced the local paper in September 1946. Other sales of fence posts and barbed wire were announced. Finally on April 3, 1947, the *Seymour Weekly Republican* announced " Freeman Field To Be Disposed Of By April 30th.".

So Freeman Field then passed into history. Over time, it has evolved into an industrial park and maintains its runways to help attract indus-

try. Even though the field was now a civilian facility, many rumors persisted about the German aircraft and other equipment buried at the field prior to its closing in 1947. This was not all that surprising because the dumping of surplus material into pits and burying it was a common practice at war's end. There really wasn't much else that could be done with a lot of it. The government tried to sell and/or give away the billions of dollars worth of military material after the war. This included everything from buildings, airplanes, mountains of parts, engines, and the everyday items found at the training bases. Think of a small city and all that it contains. The USAAF had hundreds of these small cities that were surplus virtually overnight and now had to be disposed of. There were

no funds available to maintain these bases, nor was there much desire to do anything but forget the war, and move onto a peacetime footing as soon as possible, so the Air Force, along with the other services, moved quickly to discard excess material. Ads appeared in newspapers offering everything from aircraft, to fencing, to typewriters, all at give away prices. Huge quantities of surplus material were sold to dealers and individuals, and some of it was given away to schools and local governments. Thousands of aircraft were melted down into aluminum ingots; some planes were brand new, right off the assembly line. Much of the material not sold, given away, or scrapped, was dumped into trenches and buried.

The rumors of buried material at Freeman Field made sense given its special mission late in the war. Not only were there more than a hun-

Dallas Tohill, on left and Lex Cralley setting up the ground imaging radar equipment prior to searching a possible dig site. The soil conditions, and thick brush at the former airbase proved to be a worthy opponent for the equipment.

Dallas Tohill, carrying a metal detector, accompanied by Lex Cralley working a search pattern in an attempt to locate the material.

dred German and Allied aircraft at the field, there were also warehouses filled with every kind of Luftwaffe equipment. General Arnold's order establishing Freeman Field as the test center stated that he wanted at least one example of every kind of enemy equipment. This included radars, instruments, manuals, parachutes, binoculars, combat reports, etc. Wright Field cataloged this material and maintained the file in their archives. Correspondence kept on file at the Smithsonian between Wright Field and Freeman Field confirms the existence of vast quantities of German equipment.

Since the field's closing, many people have come forward and talked about either seeing or being involved in the dumping of planes/parts at Freeman Field. One gentleman recalls his in-volvement in the burial of an aircraft while working as a civilian employee at the field. He remembers German and Japanese parts being buried at the field. He tells the story of the day a flat bed truck arrived at Freeman's gate; it had an aircraft fuselage wrapped in plastic secured to the bed of the truck. The truck was driven out to a field south and east of a runway and dumped into a large ditch, about fifty feet long. The plane or fuselage was then covered with dirt using a bulldozer. Another of the many

With the airport manager, Ted Jordan looking on, and ready to assist when necessary, Dallas Tohill is using the backhoe to remove some of the material.

The mayor of Seymour, Mr. John Burkhart visiting the dig site and looking at some of the findings of the day. The mayor's interest and support of the project were vital to its success.

A view of one pit that shows some of the material to the left. Dallas Tohill is standing, below and to the left is the author, and to the right is Lex Cralley. The large piece of material to the author's right is a radiator that was sitting on top of part of an aircraft engine. (JANE)

A view of a few propeller blades found at the site before being cleaned. Some were made of wood and in poor shape. The metal ones were in generally good condition with a few protected by cosmoline (a heavy grease).

burial stories comes from a former soldier who was stationed at the field during the period when the field was being shut down. He did various jobs including performing the duties of an M.P. He also drove truckloads of surplus material to the Jeffersonville Quartermaster Depot in Jeffersonville, Indiana. This material was salvageable items, such as refrigerators, that could be sold or perhaps used again by the military in a different location. At the end of each day, he would return to Freeman Field, park his truck, and then use a bull dozer to cover pits that had been filled with surplus equipment during the day. He specifically remembered covering an aircraft engine, and "a carload of parachute silk" with dirt. He also recalled his friend working in another part of the then deserted airfield burying equipment, but did not know specifically what was buried in that place. Another long time resident of Seymour remembers as a young boy when the military buried equipment. He would go into the area after the personnel had left for the day and dig up things, probably tools, and take them home.

There are other stories similar to these, enough to give credence to the fact that equipment was buried at Freeman Field sometime during 1945 to 1947.

Serious efforts to recover buried material began in early 1992. At the time, a group called

Part of the recovered tail section from a Fw-190, note the swastika. Next to it is a wheel cover from a Spitfire.

11

Blue Sky Aviation located in Louisville, Kentucky and headed by Charles Osborn III and his manager Ron Griffin, received permission from the airport authorities to search for buried Luftwaffe equipment that might be located on airport property. This was a vast search area consisting of about 2,200 acres, much of which was leased to farmers and under cultivation with corn or soybeans. The first area to be searched was selected based upon its proximately to the six then remaining warehouses from WW II, and information from a former GI who had worked at the field. He claimed to have witnessed material being buried in the location. It was decided to run a magnetometer survey to determine if there was any indication of buried metal. In addition to magnetometer surveys, several experts were consulted at Purdue University, Indiana State University, and Wright State University. Discussions included the nature of the soil in which the material was buried, and the various types of search techniques. By April, the preliminary work was complete. The group had strong indications, in several spots, of objects deep in the soil with significant metal content so, with hopes running high, digging began. Most of the holes dug were rather small, just large enough to determine if anything of value had been discovered with the magnetometer and/or metal detector. Some of the first holes contained junk dumped in the area during the post war years, mostly miscellaneous pieces of metal, tin cans, bottles, wire, etc, the same type of items one would find in an old dump. There was nothing found at first to indicate that field was ever used to bury anything connected with any kind of aircraft, German or otherwise. From time to time, the group would return to Freeman Field for a day or so and continue to

Part of an eight-stage compressor from a Junkers Jumo 004 engine.

dig small holes where the magnetometer indicated something with metal content was buried. The first encouraging find occurred near the site of the former base incinerator. Here, about three feet below the surface, was uncovered considerable material buried during the war; however, it was simply burned trash from the base incinerator, and in some cases, items that had been buried along with the incinerator trash. Found were small pieces of air craft parts, such as parts of destroyed instruments, newspapers dated in the forties (some were still readable), and in one spot, a small bit of fabric covering from what was assumed to be an AT-10. Also, an occasional Coke bottle dating from the forties turned up. After reviewing the findings, and the lack of success in what was thought to be a site with excellent potential, it was decided to search other areas of the field. Everyone was disappointed with the lack of results, but at this point, no one wanted to give up. Blue Sky Aviation then moved their efforts to another part of the field about a half mile from the original search area. As before, nothing was found. Mr. Osborne then decided to discontinue his efforts at Freeman Field.

The efforts to unravel the mysteries of Freeman Field lay dormant until 1995. At that time, a gentleman who had a long time interest in Freeman Field, and who had successfully recovered WW II aviation artifacts elsewhere, was quietly working with the officials of the field to obtain permission for a search. Lex Cralley, the founder of Salvage I headquartered in Princeton, Minnesota, was convinced of the existence of buried aircraft parts and perhaps entire aircraft at the field. He had patiently waited while Blue Sky Aviation was working the field.

After their search was complete, he came forward with his proposal. For Lex, the recovery of WW II aviation artifacts is a labor of love, so he spends much of his free time looking for the planes that flew long ago.

This time there was a different search methodology that included ground imaging radar. In addition, Lex believed in getting the local people involved in the search by asking them to review their memories of the field's activities in 1946 and 1947. Through this method, he found some who did remember digging activities at the field at war's end. Since his job permits only infrequent visits to the actual site, he did considerable research via phone. By August 1995, everything was ready to dig at a new site. An aerial view of the field taken after the war, along with other indications, indicated the possibility of a large trench, long since covered over, that was now part of a corn field. After making the necessary arrangements with the farmer who was using the land (Lex bought several acres of corn), a backhoe was brought in. Again, with hopes running high, the digging began in the heat and humidity of a typical Indiana summer, however; Freeman Field was not going to give up its

An interesting view of the data information found on the blade of a prop believed to be from the engine of an AT-10. This was one of the very few American parts found.

secrets easily. The dig produced nothing. After several days of exploring, mostly via small holes, it was decided that nothing was buried in that spot. Over the next several months, other areas were searched, but nothing positive was found.

By now it was early 1997; Lex was still researching possible burial spots, and Freeman Field had a new airport manager, Mr. Ted Jordan, appointed in 1995. Ted has all the right qualities for this complex job. He is a recently retired banking executive, with a strong background in management. Additionally, Ted has excellent business and public relations experience, and a deep love for all things connected

This may be part of an exhaust nozzle from a V-2 rocket engine.

with aviation, especially the history of Freeman Field. Ted balances his responsibilities to the local community, the FAA and other governmental agencies, with his interest in aviation archeology.

In the spring of 1997, the first solid evidence of buried aircraft parts was uncovered at Freeman Field. Bits and pieces for sure, but confirmation of some of the long standing rumors about the role the field played in the evaluation of foreign aircraft. By now, Lex had been joined in his search by Dallas Tohill, an aircraft historian, who works with Gerald Yagen, president of Tidewater Tech. Dallas is a veteran of twenty-two years service with the U.S. Army. He is a graduate of the Airborne, Special Forces, and Ranger schools. He also has traveled the world looking for WW II aircraft and participated in several successful searches. Gerald Yagen is an aircraft enthusiast, an accomplished pilot, and owner of Tidewater Tech, an aviation maintenance school located in Norfolk, Virginia. The school also operates their own historic aircraft restoration facility. Tidewater Tech had joined Lex as an equal partner and was making the major contribution toward financing a new and concentrated effort to locate the buried material.

It was now late August, and the search was near the old base incinerator. Some preliminary work had been done here in February - no mosquitos but lots of ice and snow. The group had learned that even using the best of search equipment, it was still necessary to dig small holes in order to confirm the presence of buried artifacts. Also learned was that one could dig a hole twelve feet deep and yet miss an object that might be just an inch away, buried to the side of the hole. This was a discouraging thought given the fact that there were about 2,200 acres, any part of which could contain the artifacts. It was literally looking for a needle in the proverbial haystack.

Finally it happened. Dallas and Lex had been digging small exploratory holes for about three days in late August and had found nothing except junk buried during the fifties and sixties, the same mixture of old tin cans, bottles, an occasional tire, or piece of steel. Everyone was feeling more than a little discouraged, and miserable from the late August heat, mosquito bites, and poison ivy rash. They decided to dig in another spot about five feet away from a previous hole, and there it was. Not more than three feet below the surface, the back hoe uncovered the most beautiful engine cylinder head in the world! Additional digging brought almost a hundred cylinder heads, many from different engines. Continued digging in a north easterly direction turned up propeller blades, some clearly from an FW 190, two from an AT-10 and others not yet identified. Also hugh wooden props, with some kind of number written on them were uncovered. The condition of the metal props was extremely good. We found one, still in cosmoline (a thick protective grease), with several names scratched into the grease. One read "J. M. Muldoon, 550 Grah (last letter unreadable), Bky NY." This was probably written by a GI or civilian employee of the sub-depot just before the material was transported to the dump site.

At this point, it was very difficult to use the back hoe for fear of damaging the parts. It appeared that the parts had been loaded on the back of a truck, transported to the site, and simply dumped. By now, Lex and Dallas were running into parts of aircraft, such as wheel faring doors (a least one from a Spitfire), landing gear struts, German aircraft tires, instruments (mostly radio equipment, some with their Luftwaffe data plates) , and engine parts. Also found was most of a vertical tail grouping from an FW-190. Some of the paint was well preserved with part of the Swastika easily visible. Thankfully, the weather had been very dry over the summer and there was little water to contend with. Normally, the water table is high in this part of Indiana. Some of the parts were as deep as twelve feet, others lay just below the surface. It was difficult digging because it was done in mid eighty degree heat with a high humidity that was most uncomfortable. The mosquitos were especially thick because the area was in thick brush. In some cases, it was necessary to remove the parts by hand. Often, they

Ted Jordan standing next to the entrance sign for the Freeman Field museum. This growing museum is located in two former WWII buildings and contains memorabilia from the field's history and displays various items of the former training base.

were laying on top of each other, weighed down by 50 years of settling, the weight of the other parts, and several feet of mud, The parts were packed so closely together, that much had to be removed by hand. Only the thrill of finding this wonderful treasure of Luftwaffe material made up for the oppressive heat and constant unwanted attention from the bug population of southern Indiana. Later, Lex would have to visit the hospital for treatment of a severe case of poison ivy coupled with mosquito bites.

By now, the pit was about 50 feet long, 50 feet wide and ranged in depth from 2 to 12 feet. One puzzling thing was that no jet engine or aircraft parts had been found. The research indicated Luftwaffe jets were on the field. Also, we clearly had hit what was a dump site for parts from the old Freeman Field engineering shops. We knew work was performed on the jets while

they were at the field. If so, where were the parts? The insidious nature of this dig soon came to light. The parts were found in a separate pit not more than 15 feet away from the now growing hole that contained the piston engine parts. One of the better finds was an eight-stage compressor from a Junker Jumo 004 engine, the same type of engine that powered the Me 262.

After several years of painstaking, expensive, and sometimes frustrating research and exploration, the existence of buried German aircraft parts at Freeman Field was finally proven. The amount of buried material recovered is quite large and exceptionally interesting, however, still persisting, is the rumor that unopened crates of Luftwaffe material are buried somewhere on the field. If these crates do exist, their contents will prove to be of significant value to museums all over the world. So, the search continues.

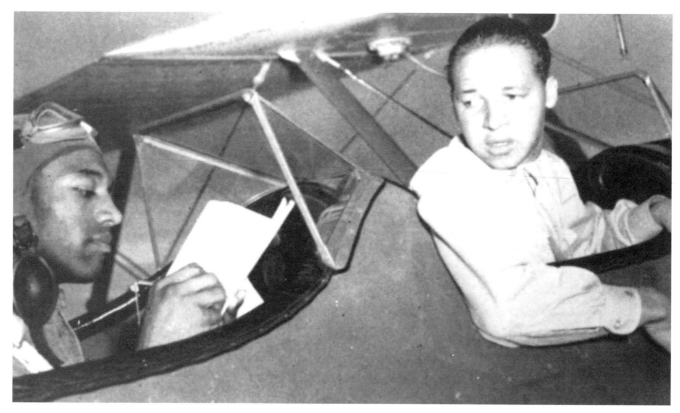

Mr. Sherman Rose is the instructor in the front seat during discussion with a cadet who is taking notes.

(ARMY AND NAVY PUBLISHING CO., INC.)

A group of Moton Field mechanics standing among their trainers. (ARMY AND NAVY PUBLISHING CO., INC.)

2

Birth of the Tuskegee Airmen

MOTON FIELD

The training of the first African-Americans for eventual duty as pilots in the United States Air Force began in the small, rural town of Tuskegee, Alabama. In 1941, the United States Army Air Corps called this training "The Tuskegee Experiment." Others, including some who took the training, would refer to it as "an experiment designed to fail."

Long before the training of blacks could begin at Moton Field many problems, some which seemed insurmountable, had to be solved. Not the least of which was the fact that as late as 1939 blacks were excluded from military flying. The reason was prejudice. At the time, the military simply reflected general society; there were few black American civilian pilots just as there were few black bus drivers, train engineers, police officers, store managers, elected officials, or long distance truck drivers. In short, most blacks found only menial work. But, there were others who believed that given the opportunity blacks could do just as well as anyone else, they just needed a chance. It is to the credit of the military that in many cases, some of its members put aside the traditional thinking of the day and allowed blacks the opportunity.

Over time, black Americans would get their chance to fly military aircraft. That time came

on March 7, 1942, when the first five black Americans attended a graduation exercise in the brisk March air on the runway of Tuskegee Army Air Field. They received their wings as pilots in the United States Army Air Forces.

Before that graduation exercise took place, however, laws had to be passed, legal battles fought, and attitudes changed. Also, the ever present specter of prejudice and segregation would constantly overshadow the program and provide a fertile environment to deny black Americans this opportunity; however, progress was slowly made. The first step came in 1938 with the passing of the Civilian Pilot Training Act Program (CPTP). This program had as its purpose the training of civilian pilots to create a reserve that could be called upon for further military training as pilots in the event of a national emergency. About 400,000 pilots received their civilian pilot's license under this program, and about 2,700 of these were black Americans. The first six black schools enrolled in this program were West Virginia State College, Delaware State College, Hampton Institute, Howard University, North Carolina Agricultural and Technical College, and Tuskegee Institute. At first, the Army Air Corps refused to accept any of the black graduates for enlistment, even though their graduation rate was the same as the white candidates.

Aerial view of Moton Field taken in late 1996. Buildings in left center of photo include several from the original field. Hangar No. 1 is on the right of the group and the remains of Hangar No. 2 are across from No. 1. All that remains from the second hangar is the control tower. (DAVE)

The next law which proved helpful in assuring that black Americans would be allowed to qualify for military flight training was Public Law 18. Passed in 1939, it formalized a program of aviation schools that were designed to train military aviation cadets in the elementary and primary phases of aviation. The schools would be run by civilians and funded by the government. The law also directed that one school be designated "for the training of any Negro air pilot." Still, serious problems existed with the acceptance of black Americans in the Air Corps. This was made clear by a memo written in mid 1940 by General Arnold, chief of the Air Corps. The memo noted that blacks could be used "in labor battalions or labor companies to perform the duties of post fatigue and as waiters in our messes." It also said, " Negro pilots cannot be used in our present Air Corps units since this would result in having Negro officers serving over white enlisted men. This would create an impossible social problem." General Arnold's statement was a reflection of society as it existed in 1940. Shortly after General Arnold's statement another law, the Selective Service Act, was passed in September 1940. This law helped alleviate the problem somewhat, because it required the services to accept blacks; however, segregation would still be enforced just as it was in society as a whole. An in-depth study, *Blacks In The Army Air Forces During World War II*, by Alan Osur notes: "Throughout the war, AAF commanders demonstrated a reluctance to treat blacks with full equality and to show a sincere commitment to abide by War Department racial directives." In his conclusion, Mr. Osur points out, "There is no question that during World War II the Army Air Forces (AAF) made some headway toward improved race relations; however, that partial success does not alter the fact that the AAF failed to develop a comprehensive policy for dealing with all the problems that arose following the introduction of large numbers of black soldiers. . . . The AAF and the War Department operated under the official policy of segregation in terms of housing, messing, and recreation; since they considered these facilities 'separate-but-equal,' they did not find their policy discriminatory. Unfortunately, the system reflected the racist tradition of American society, and despite sincere and wholehearted efforts by some commanders in actual practice, the military did not grant blacks equal treatment. As a result, from the perspective of the black soldier, segregation was unacceptable, and from the perspective of the AAF, it was not efficient."

The story of Moton Field starts at the Municipal Airport in Montgomery, Alabama. Here in December 1939 or January 1940, flight training started for those enrolled in the Civilian Pilot Training Program at the Tuskegee Institute. Flight training was carried out in Montgomery, about forty miles from the Institute, because the school itself had no airfield. This site required a waiver because contracts required the airfield be located within ten miles from the school; however, thanks to the efforts of Professor G.L. Washington and the understanding of the CAA, the waiver was

A good view of Hangar No.1 as it appeared in late 1996. Note the brick construction. The other hangar was like this and destroyed by fire sometime in 1989.

A rear view of Hangar No. 1 taken in 1995.

granted. [The CAA was the Civil Aeronautics Authority, forerunner of today's FAA] Professor Washington, a black, was a graduate of the Massachusetts Institute of Technology and was head of the Department of Mechanical Industries, Division of Aeronautics at Tuskegee. At first, flight instruction was done by pilots from the Alabama Polytechnic Institute, today's Auburn University. Several months later, flight training was transferred to a small field that was built near the Tuskegee Institute. This field was called Field No.1, or Kennedy Field. The first CPTP class from the Tuskegee Institute received their civilian pilot licenses in May 1940.

Over time the Tuskegee Institute earned the right to give secondary (advanced) flight instruc-

tion under the CPTD program. By early 1941, the school was certified by the Civil Aeronautics Administration to give courses in civil pilot training, consisting of Elementary, Secondary, and Secondary Instructor training. This was an indication of the quality of the graduates of the Tuskegee program, and the commitment of the Institute to train black Americans for a career in aviation. After many months of effort by leaders in the black community to encourage the Air Corps to allow blacks the opportunity to fly, the War Department was forced to form an all black pursuit squadron. Later, this was called the 99th Pursuit Squadron, and it would be the first all black combat unit in Air Corps history. It was decided that the Tuskegee Institute would receive the contract for the primary training. The basic and advanced training would take place at a field, yet to be built, about seven miles from the town of

The original entrance to Moton Field. In front of the brick columns was the gate house which controlled entry. A small statue of Robert Russa Moton stood in one of the column's alcoves.

cided to use the already existing buildings at the nearby Tuskegee Institute. The primary students would live at the Institute and would use its recreational and medical facilities. Also, ground school would be conducted at the Institute. The cadets would be transported from the Institute to the field for their flying lessons.

The construction of Moton Field began in early June 1941 by Archie A. Alexander, a black engineer and building contractor from Des Moines, Iowa. He had considerable difficulty getting specific information and direction from the Army about construction of the field, so details of the construction site, buildings etc. were worked out between Professor Washington, and Mr. Alexander. Additionally, the number of cadets assigned to the field by the War Department for its first class (42-C) changed several times. Twelve cadets and Captain Benjamin O. Davis made up the first class. Not helping the situation was the attitude of the people of Tuskegee. Many viewed this "experiment" with hostility, suspicion, and amusement. It was their feeling that blacks lacked the intelligence and talent to fly; they resented their status as cadets and/or officers, and thought the whole program was a

Tuskegee. The Institute would be required to build a new training field for the primary training of cadets, and it would be called Field # 2, or Moton Field. The field was named to honor Dr. Robert Russa Moton, the second President of Tuskegee Institute.

The first site selected for the field was near the small town of Hardaway, Alabama about 15 miles south and west of Tuskegee; however, the soil was not suitable for landings, and since it was distant from the Institute, a different spot was chosen. It was finally decided to build on a site of about 650 acres owned by Mr. Eich that was about 3 miles northeast of the city of Tuskegee. Some of the land was used for growing corn and cotton. Facilities at the field would be basic because it was de-

The author's son (a USAF- F-16 pilot) standing in front of the present day manager's office. Today the field is managed by Col. R. J. Lewis USAF (Ret.).

20

A small memorial with a flag pole that stands in tribute to the men who served at Moton Field. The memorial is located in the parking lot near the present day manager's office. The plaque reads "This plaque is in honor of Black airmen trained in Tuskegee, Alabama who gave their lives in the service of their country. Dedicated at Tuskegee Municipal Airport Moton Field, 4 October, 1974."

waste of money. The town of Tuskegee was characterized by Colonel Parrish (first commander of Moton Field) as "openly hostile to all Negroes throughout the war." There would be no offers from the town of Tuskegee of financial aid or inducements to build the flying school. Most of the money needed to build the field came from the Rosenwald Fund of Chicago which had as a member of their board, Mrs. Eleanor Roosevelt. She later became a supporter of black aviation and the Tuskegee school. While on a visit to the Tuskegee Campus in 1941, she was taken for a ride in one of the school's Piper Cubs by Chief Anderson, over the objections of her Secret Service escort. It is reported that the agents phoned the President in an attempt to stop her, but Mr. Roosevelt said to the effect, "she will do what she wants to do." This was unheard of, the wife of the President of the United States taken for a flight in a small, single engine aircraft flown by a black aviator. It was after the flight, that the fund lent much of the money that was needed for construction of the field.

Because the cadets would attend ground

Another building remaining on the field today is the All Ranks Club. It was used for recreation by cadets, instructors, officers, and civilians. Here they could enjoy a soft drink, have a hot dog, use the library, play Ping Pong, or read.

school and live at the Tuskegee Institute during their primary training, it was necessary to convert several buildings on the campus. This included the conversion of the Boy's Bath House for a barracks, and two rooms in another building (Phelps Hall) for classrooms. On the airfield site, land had to be cleared of trees, and the airstrip graded and compacted. Since this was a primary field there would be no runways

Still remaining from its WW II use is the Locker Building. Its main purpose was to serve as a bathing facility for the cadets and perhaps workers at the field, and a restroom for the men and women working on the field.

as such, just a large level field able to support the light weight of the trainers in use at the time. Sewers had to be installed, and a source of water found, because the town of Tuskegee did not furnish a water supply. Water was obtained from springs near hangar #1. Additional construction began in June 1942, and included a second hangar, with a control tower, a supply building, a bath and locker building, and some other small buildings. The field was about 45% complete by December 1942, even though it had been in use for over a year. The Tuskegee students helped build and maintain the buildings at the field. The two hangars were impressive structures, and were made of brick. In total, Moton Field had about 15 buildings.

The field was formally opened on July 19,

1941 during a ceremony held on the Tuskegee Institute campus in front of the Booker T. Washington monument. Several dignitaries attended including Brigadier General Walter Weaver, Commander General of the Southeast Training Center, Dr. Frederick Patterson, President of Tuskegee Institute, Captain Noel Parrish, Commander of Moton Field, and Mr. Hillard Robinson, the architect at Tuskegee Institute. Several telegrams of congratulations were received, including those from General George Marshall and General Henry Arnold. Also on the stand was Captain Benjamin O. Davis Jr, a member of the first class and a West Point graduate. He would be the first black man to officially solo an aircraft as an officer of the Army Air Corps.

The first class started their pre-flight training on July 20, and began flight training around August 21. When flight training began, the planes had to be flown over each day from Kennedy Field, (about four miles south of Tuskegee) and returned to Kennedy Field each night. Later, around September 1, flight training was moved to Moton Field. Even at this late date, conditions were still primitive. The offices had not been completed, windows were not in, nor were screens installed to keep out the flies, mosquitoes, and other bugs that were so troublesome. Captain Parrish purchased a bottle of citronella to help ward off the insects. There was no office equipment, so a typist's chair was borrowed, and a table made to be used as a typist's desk. As of November 1, there was not a telephone at the flying field.

Flight training required expert maintenance to help offset the rough usage of the planes by the cadets. One of the mechanics at Moton Field was Bill Childs who started as a mechanic's helper at Kennedy Field in July 1942. Later he moved to Moton Field where he worked in hangar #2 repairing major components, such as repairing en-

All that remains of Hangar No. 2. The three story structure in the right of the picture is what's left of the control tower and parachute loft. The cleared area to the left of the tower is the floor for the former hangar.

gines, and changing wings. He remembers working an eight-hour day. He was honored to be there because of the concentrated assembly of black brain power, and the capabilities of the men undergoing flight training. Eventually Bill would become a licensed mechanic, earning the coveted Aircraft and Engine Mechanic rating. He recalls the Ryan PT-22 did not last long because it was too fragile to handle the hard usage of pilots learning to fly. He also remembers that the flying program had failure built in. Too often, he saw good potential flying officers washed out, some on their final check ride, simply because, at the time, Tuskegee AAF could not graduate a greater percentage of pilots than the white schools.

At first, all the flight instructors were white pilots. Later, after the first class had moved on for further training at Tuskegee Army Air Field, the white flight instructors at Moton Field were replaced with black instructors. Heading up the group of black flight instructors at Moton Field was Mr. Charles Alfred Anderson, who would become famous in his own right for his uncompromising adherence to excellence, and his role in the training of the Tuskegee Airmen. He would be affectionately known as "Chief." Prior to his becoming head of the flight instructors at Moton, Chief Anderson and his group were responsible for instructing the CPTD students in the advanced course of flying at Tuskegee Institute. Mr.

Anderson was born in 1907, purchased his first airplane in 1928, and by the age of 25 had his Air Transport License. He was from Bryn Mawr, Pennsylvania, and had about 3,500 flying hours before his appointment as chief instructor for the primary students. He and his staff would train many, including America's first black four star general, General Daniel "Chappie" James.

Primary flight school was a twelve (1939), ten (1940), or nine (1942) week course depending upon the needs of the Air Forces at the time. It consisted of periods of ground school mixed in with flight training. Normally, ground school was conducted in the morning and flying in the afternoon, or vice versa, depending on the class size, weather, availability of aircraft, etc. Generally speaking, there were four phases of flying instruction. This included pre-solo, then instruction in more complex flying procedures and later, work on elements such as precision landing and approaches, and finally aerobatics. The first class to receive instruction in the Link Trainer was class 42-K. Depending upon the availability of the trainer(s) and time, students received from two to six hours instruction. Some cadets may have received none.

Mr. Ed (Don) Doram is a Tuskegee Airman, Class 44-I who recalls that his primary training lasted 12 weeks. While taking primary training, he lived in a dormitory on the Tuskegee Institute campus, and his day started early. He was up at 5:00 A.M., and did physical training, then he had a quick breakfast. After that, and a change in uniform, was off to flying training. Generally, his flying training was in the morning and ground school was in the afternoon. The course wasn't easy, as indicated by the fact that about 20% of Don's class of 75 cadets failed. The trainer used in his class was the PT-19; however, earlier classes flew the PT-13 and also the PT-17. In total, Don enjoyed his flight training. Even though he was part of the historic first group of black flying officers, he never felt like a crusader. He just wanted to serve his country and not spend the duration in some backwater army post doing menial labor. By flying in combat, he would be in control of his own fate, because in the sky, it was skill that counted, not color.

In short, the life of the cadet was physically and emotionally draining. It also could be dangerous. During the course of the war, 439 cadets were killed in primary flight training nationwide, and 1032 trainers wrecked. Added to the everyday stress of learning to fly, mastering the ground school subjects, and avoiding demerits for any number of reasons, was the fear of the "washout." This was a term for failing a course of instruction, or not being able to develop the necessary flying skills in the short time allocated. A cadet's flying career was over if he washed out. Another emotional and physical strain on the cadets was the practice of hazing by the upperclassmen. Praised by some, condemned by others, it was felt the practice helped a cadet develop military bearing, discipline, or other positive traits. Regardless, it certainly added to a cadet's misery.

Don chuckles when he recalls his hazing by the upperclassmen. On occasion, an upper class cadet would storm into the barracks and require the lower class cadet to memorize five or six short phrases written on a piece of paper. They were usually given about twenty minutes to accomplish this task. To make it more interesting, there was only one sheet of paper to be shared by the thirty or so cadets in the barracks. One saying Don memorized went like this: "Sir!, my head is made of Vermont marble and African Ivory covered by a thick layer of case hardened steel, hence the somniferous and ostentatiously and effervescent phrases so reiterated and directed for my comprehension have failed to penetrate this atrocious intelligence—in short sir, I am very dumb and do not understand." Godfrey Miller another Tuskegee Airman, Class of 45 H, remembers a different hazing practice called "Air Raid/Flood" Training. In this instance, an upperclassman would rush into the barracks and yell "Air Raid." Then, the cadets would have to leap from their bunks or wherever they were, and crawl under the lower bunk of the two tier bunk bed. If the upperclassman yelled "Flood" then the cadets would have to rush to climb onto the upper bunk.

For many cadets, their first airplane ride was

A night view of the interior of a Moton Field hangar. (AF HISTORICAL RESEARCH AGENCY, CAVER)

Mechanics at work steam cleaning one of the training planes. (AF HISTORICAL RESEARCH AGENCY, CAVER)

during primary training at Moton Field. John Leahr, Class 43-G, remembers his well. It was love at first flight, and unlike many others, he never became airsick. John's first solo in the PT-17 trainer was almost his last. After given clearance by his instructor for the solo, John taxied to the take off area. After doing his flight checks, running up the engine, and clearing the area for other aircraft he gunned the engine for the take off run. He had reached an altitude of about fifteen feet when he heard a strange noise. Looking up, he saw that another aircraft was descending directly on top of his plane. He immediately cut power and nosed the aircraft down. The other plane must have seen his at the same instant and applied power and climbed to avoid the crash. The corrective measures were not quite fast enough, and the prop of John's plane hit the tail wheel of the other. There was a loud cracking sound. After landing, John looked at his instructor at the other end of the field expecting a signal to return back to the flight line.

There was no signal, so John realized that his instructor was not aware that there had been contact with the other craft. The other plane had climbed and was circling in the traffic pattern. John felt that when the other plane landed and they became aware of the accident, his flying career would be over. So with his prop damaged, he took off, determined to finish his first solo flight; however, the prop was damaged, and as a result, he had to use full stick and rudder to keep his plane from going into a roll. He climbed and circled the field. The other plane landed, and soon the ground personnel became aware of the incident. After the field was cleared, he made a good landing using full rudder and aileron to keep the plane under control. His instructor came over to inspect John's prop after he had cut the engine. There was a rather large nick in the prop blade, so the airplane was returned to the hangar for repair. John was ordered to report to the field commander for what he thought would be the end of his cadet career, but

A close up view of a cadet and an instructor in the cockpit. Note that the instructor (in front) seems to be talking to the cadet. This is a good picture of the infamous Gosport tube communication system. This was strictly a one way communication device. The instructor talked into the tube in front while the student could hear through the tube which was connected to the earholes in his flight helmet. (ARMY AND NAVY PUBLISHING CO., INC.)

at least he had the satisfaction that goes with a pilot's first solo. Much to his surprise, his only penalty was a good tongue lashing. After graduation and earning his wings, John joined the 332nd fighter Group and flew 132 combat missions in the P-39, P-47, and the P-51.

Don Doram took his first flight in a Piper Cub while attending Preflight training at the Tuskegee Institute. His instructor was Mr. Jackson who had a mirror in the cockpit by which he was able to watch his passenger's reactions to their flight. He gave Don a thorough wringing out in the Cub to determine Don's aptitude for unusual attitudes and general comfort level in an aircraft. This included steep turns, stalls, and whatever else the little Cub could do. Don took it all in stride and thought it quite fun. He passed the test, and was advised by Mr. Jackson that he would do quite well in his future flight training.

Most of the USAAF cadets who took flight training were subjected to fatigue, emotional strain, accelerated training, and the ever present fear of the dreaded washout. The cadets at

Moton Field, and later Tuskegee Army Air Field, had another obstacle to face—prejudice. John Leahr had lived with it all his life. Still he was upset when as a youth and on a visit to the local airport for a Senior Career Day, the person speaking to his group, looked at John, the only black in the group, and said "There was no place in aviation for Negroes. " Later on, while wearing the uniform of a commissioned officer in the United States Army Air Forces, he would be beaten and have his life threatened on different occasions by racial bigots. Don Doram especially remembers the train ride from his home in Cincinnati, Ohio to the deep south. Because he was black, he was required to take his meals in the dining car sitting alone at a table that was screened from the other occupants of the car.

According to the history of the 66th AAF Flying Training Detachment, there was not much interest shown by the Headquarters, Southeast Air Corps Training Center in Moton Field. The history reports:

"As a matter of fact, Headquarters, Southeast Air Corps Training Center, Maxwell Field, Alabama paid little attention to this installation in the early days of its operation, because it was looked upon as a sort of experiment. In the beginning, no one took the project too seriously. As training progressed and classes were turned out, Headquarters, Southeast was so pleased to see that proficient pilots were being developed, that they were more than content to let the program ride along undisturbed. In other words, during the first six months or more of progress, the detachment received almost no visitors and almost no inspectors. The reason for so few visitors from Headquarters, Southeast was believed to be that they were all a little wary of the racial aspects of the program, and it appeared that they were actually a little reluctant to interest themselves in something which they knew little or nothing about."

Captain Noel Parrish, a white officer and the first commander of Moton Field, remembers the town of Tuskegee as "openly hostile to all Negroes throughout the war." In many ways it was like so many other southern towns, rigidly segregated with virtually no entertainment facilities for the black cadets undergoing training at Moton Field. When Benjamin O. Davis, later to rise to the rank of three star general, was assigned to the Tuskegee Institute in 1938 as professor of military science and tactics, he was again faced with the prejudice of this small town. He recalls that his wife would import clothes from New York and sell them at a small profit to women who

were unable to find similar clothes in Tuskegee. At the time, blacks were not allowed to try on clothing, hats, or shoes in the white-owned stores in the area. He also recalls an ugly incident in a Tuskegee post office when a black patron was slapped by the postmaster for refusing to give up his place in the waiting line for a white patron. So to avoid any trouble, some of the cadets simply avoided the town and the people in it. Godfrey Miller, who would go on to finish his training at Tuskegee Army Air Field, and serve twenty years in the Air Force retiring as a Lt. Colonel, was one of those who avoided the town. He did not go into Tuskegee because he was afraid of how he would react to the racism there. It was much worse and less subtle than what he had experienced back home in Illinois. Godfrey felt, however, that his training was excellent and was never slighted because of his race.

As mentioned, the first commanding officer of the training detachment was Captain Noel F. Parrish, who reported for duty and assumed command on July 19, 1941. He served here until December 3, 1941, and at that time was replaced by Lt. William T. Smith who was in charge until November 18, 1943. He was followed by

A cadet landing his aircraft while the instructor on the ground is observing and grading the exercise.

(U.S. AIR FORCE MUSEUM)

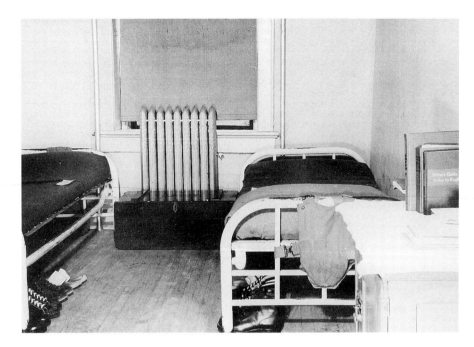

A view of a cadet's room. The cadets lived on the campus of the Tuskegee Institute. Note the rather spartan conditions.

(AF HISTORICAL RESEARCH AGENCY, CAVER)

Major Harold C. Magoon who was on the original staff of officers. The first class, 42-C, consisted of thirteen men, twelve cadets and one student officer, Captain Benjamin O. Davis. Of the thirteen men, six completed the primary training and five would earn their wings. While the failure rate seemed high, it was generally in line with the Air Corps washout rate at the time, 50% to 60%; however, the potential aviators were further hampered by a quota system which delayed and sometimes prevented qualified black men from entering the flight training program. Often, the waiting list was so long that many qualified blacks were drafted into other parts of the military while waiting the opportunity to begin cadet training. Additional comments on the failure rate were made by Captain Parrish. He felt that improvements could be made in the method of cadet selection. He noted among other things, that the selection of candidates be based upon some indication of prior demonstration of superior ability rather than upon priority of application or other meaningless bases. During 1943, the percentage of washouts for Moton Field was about 36%, this compares with 28% for the entire Eastern Flying Training Command.

The first five black men to receive their wings as pilots in the United States Army Air Forces were Benjamin Davis, Lemuel Custis, Charles Debow, Mac Ross, and Spencer (Spanky) Roberts. As a member of the 99th Fighter Squadron, Captain Lemuel Custis, was credited with shooting down a Macchi 205 in January 27, 1944. Captain Charles Debow went on to become commander of the 301st Fighter Squadron. Captain Mac Ross would pay the supreme price when he died in a plane crash in Italy on July 12, 1944. Major Spanky Roberts was awarded the Distinguished Flying Cross. He also became commander of the famed 99th Fighter Squadron and later commander of the 332nd Fighter Group. The role Benjamin Davis played in Air Force history is legendary. He spent nearly thirty-five years in the military, retiring in 1970 as a three star general. His last command was Deputy Commander-in-Chief, U.S. Strike Command at MacDill Air Force Base. His awards include the Silver Star, Distinguished Flying Cross, and the Croix de Guerre.

The Tuskegee Airmen who flew with the 99th Fighter Squadron and the 332nd Fighter Group had an impressive combat record. In spite of second hand equipment, and the continuing reluctance of the military to accept them as full partners, they destroyed or damaged 409 enemy aircraft in the air or on the ground. In their role as a ground attack unit, they destroyed or damaged numerous ground targets including 619 box cars and other railroad rolling stock, plus 126 locomotives. Not satisfied with ground targets in their strafing missions, Captain Wendell Pruitt and Lieutenant Gwynne Pierson sank a German Destroyer. Flying as bomber escorts, the pilots of

Aerial view of Tuskegee Army Air Field as it appeared in July 1945. This was generally the next step for the cadets after finishing their training at Moton Field. Today little remains and it is sometimes called Sharps Field after the sand and gravel company which operates on the former air base. (U.S. AIR FORCE MUSEUM)

the 332nd Fighter Group never lost a bomber to the action of enemy fighters. After the war, pilots from the 332nd Fighter Group won the first ever USAF Fighter Gunnery Meet (reciprocating type aircraft—F-47's) held at Las Vegas Air Force Base (Nellis Air Force Base) in May 1949.

The last primary class to graduate Moton Field, did so on November 23, 1945. There were about 2400 students who started their training here. Today, Moton Field is the Tuskegee Municipal Airport, and still serves as a jumping off spot for fledgling aviators in its role as a general aviation airport. It now has a 5000-foot asphalt runway in place of the grass landing field where so many cadets made their flights in PT-13's, PT-17's, PT-19's, and the PT-22; however, visitors to this historic field will find that much remains from its World War II service. About nine of the fifteen original buildings remain including hangar #1, the All Ranks Club, part of the control tower, and the locker building. Much of the original entrance that contained a bust of Robert Russa Moton is still here alongside the road that leads to the hangars. There is a small memorial

29

here that reads: "This plaque is in honor of black airmen trained in Tuskegee, Alabama who gave their lives in the service of their country. Dedicated at Tuskegee Municipal Airport, Moton Field, 4 October 1974."

In October 1998, Congress passed legislation that established Moton Field as the Tuskegee Airmen National Historic Site, and a new unit of the National Park System. This action gives honor to and helps commemorate the role of the Tuskegee Airman. As a final note, it is important to remember that not all black army pilots earned their wings at Tuskegee Army Air Field. Some pilots such as Charles "Briggie" Brown were commissioned officers in the field artillery at Fort Sill, Oklahoma in 1942, and then sent for flight training. Some received training at Tuskegee Army Air Field, while others did so at Pittsburgh, Kansas, or Denton, Texas. After completing flight training they returned to Fort Sill for further training in artillery spotting. After that, they served as Liaison pilots for the United States Army.

This is what's left of Tuskegee Army Air Field today. The outlines of the former streets, aircraft parking ramp and traffic circle are clearly visible. (DAVE)

Another view of the former field, showing the ramp and part of the runway system. What remains of the field is slowly being obscured by brush and trees.   (DAVE)

3

Primary Training

CARLSTROM FIELD

Located about fifty air miles north and east of Fort Myers, Florida, near the town of Arcadia, are the sites of two former Army Air Forces primary training airfields, Carlstrom and Dorr Fields. These complexes turned out thousands of fledgling pilots during both World War I and World War II.

The story of World War II primary training is interesting for many reasons, one of which is the fact that the training was handled by civilians guided by military supervision. It was in May 1939 that nine civilian flying schools got the go ahead from the Air Corps to start training in July. From the nine original schools, the program grew to its peak in 1943 with fifty-six civilian pilot training schools. The high point in terms of graduates was reached in November 1943, when 11,411 aviation cadets were graduated and entered basic flying school. Over time, as the desperate need for pilots eased, the civilian pilot schools were gradually closed, and by the end of 1944, just ten schools remained in use.

Why did the military need civilians to handle the primary training? It was a simple matter of time and expediency. Thanks to the failure of our politicians to adequately fund the military over many years following World War I, we found ourselves totally unprepared to defend freedom in a

Left to right are Ken Povey, civilian manager of Carlstrom Field, John Paul Riddle-owner, Col. William Welsch, commander of the South East Training Command, Cap. George Ola, and Brig. Gen. Barton K. Yount standing next to the cadet swimming pool. (OLA)

Right: An aerial view of Carlstrom Field circa 1943. Off to the left of the photo can be seen the remains of the original Carlstrom Field used from 1918 to 1921. The white squares along the road are the foundations for the WW I hangars. (OLA)

Below: A closer view of Carlstrom Field during WWII. Note the size of the hangars and the efficient arrangement of the training facilities. The swimming pool, tennis, and basketball courts are in the center of the photo. (OLA)

The civilian contract training program was quite extensive, multifaceted, and evolved over time. In general, the government required the primary school owners to provide the civilian instructors, facilities, and much of the equipment for training. The aircraft, textbooks, parachutes, flying clothes, and some other things were supplied by the government. At first, the government paid the civilian contractor $1,170 for each graduate, and $18.00 for each flying hour given to cadets who washed out. Later, much of this changed and is detailed as follows in Volume VI of *The Army Air Forces in World War II*:

"In July 1940 contracts were modified slightly by lowering the standard compensation for each graduate to $1,050 and to $17.50 per flying hour for eliminees. After Pearl Harbor it was necessary for the government to increase the pay of the contractors in order to allow for more extensive guard service. Later, too, the government agreed to furnish gasoline, oil, and lubricants. When the program ended, the government

world gone mad. We needed thousands of pilots, and we needed them now. The plan was to ask civilian pilot school owners to train new pilots in the entry level (primary training), and then send the graduates on to basic and later advanced training. Basic and advanced training would be handled by the military. With this program, the Air Corps (later the Army Air Forces) could focus time and energy on expanding the basic and advanced training programs, and also build the training centers needed to accomplish the more complex training.

Carlstrom Field as it appears today. It is interesting to compare this picture with the one taken during WW II and noting how much remains. Many buildings still remain including two hangars, some of the barracks (in the center of the photo), and the headquarters building.

was paying $10.00 per hour of instruction at some schools, and somewhat more at others. The government also decided, shortly after Pearl Harbor, to have the Defense Plant Corporation purchase all land, buildings, hangars, and unmovable equipment. The contractor retained ownership of what was left and paid the Defense Plant corporation a rent of $3.70 for each hour of instruction and $1.15 daily for each cadet's quarters."

When the program started in July 1939, it was structured to last twelve weeks. In May 1940, as the need for pilots became more urgent, it was cut to ten weeks, and in early 1942, nine weeks. Flying time for all the programs was sixty hours; the cuts were made in the ground school part of the training. At first, there were 225 hours of ground school, but by early 1942, this had been reduced to 84 hours. At this time, much of the ground-school was being handled in the preflight phase of pilot training. Also, some ground school training was probably eliminated in an attempt to increase the production of pilots. Later in the war, March 1944, as the need for pilots became less urgent, the training time for primary training was increased from nine to ten weeks. Overall, the program was a huge success. In 1944, General Arnold commented, "We could not possibly have trained so many airmen so quickly without these schools."

Carlstrom Field was not only one of the earliest, it was also one of the best primary training fields. The training center received its first class

of 49 cadets in March 1941, nine months before the start of World War II. This first class was 41-H, and would begin formal training on March 21, 1941. At the time, the field was under the command of Captain Stanley Donovan, a West Point graduate who took aviation training at Kelly and Randolph fields. The flying training at Carlstrom was the responsibility of the Embry Riddle Corporation. Carlstrom Field was one of six civilian contract primary flying schools that became part of the Arnold Scheme flight training program, announced in April 1941. At these schools, British student pilots would be trained alongside American cadets. The first ninety-nine British pilot cadets arrived in Arcadia during June 1941. The "Arnold Scheme" was one of many programs that helped train about 21,000 airmen from thirty-one foreign countries in flying and technical schools from May 1941 through the end of 1945.

The story of Carlstrom Field begins in 1917, when the field was built to train flyers for the first World War. Here John Paul Riddle, later to operate several civilian training schools, received flight training as a cadet. Eventually the field was closed, and over a number of years fell into disrepair. With the need for pilots becoming clear, the new Carlstrom Field was built within sight of its former World War I location. In the *Cadet's*

Col. George Ola flying over the field with his flight surgeon Dr. Sidney Nethery during the period when the field was under construction in 1941. The barracks are plainly visible in the center of the photo as is the dinning hall, the lone building on the extreme left of the picture just inside the circle road. The hospital is on the extreme right under the Steerman's tail. Also visible is the canteen which is across from the hangars inside the circle road. The headquarters is on the opposite end of the row of barracks with the road leading to it. (OLA)

Handbook issued to the newly arrived trainees at Carlstrom Field, the World War I site of the field was described as "A part of what is probably one of the finest God-made airports in the world, a spot known geographically as 'Big Prairie' which is an almost perfect landing field about 30 miles wide and 70 miles long ."

Carlstrom Field was named to honor, Victor Carlstrom, an Air Corps pilot who was killed in a plane crash. It, and the nearby Dorr Field, was built by C. F. Wheeler, a contractor from Miami, Florida. The field was dedicated on April 5, 1941 with an impressive ceremony that included a rodeo given by the then cowboy town of Arcadia, Florida. Also, a part of the opening celebration was a dance held for the cadets and others in the mess hall. When first opened, the field was quite impressive, even though it was still unfinished. When the first class of cadets arrived, it had a barren look, as the lawns had not grown in from their seeding, and some of the palm trees had just been planted the day before. Among the many buildings were two large metal hangars that would help house the brand new Stearman PT-17's flown in from the Boeing plant at Wichita, Kansas. Later, there would be five of the large hangars along with the other buildings added to accommodate the growing number of cadets.

Carlstrom was unlike most of the primary training fields because of its excellent construction, living conditions, and facilities for recreation. Many called it a "country club." Rightfully so, when compared with the spartan conditions existing at most of the bases built in haste to prepare for World War II. Instead of wood framed temporary type barracks, with no running water, and open bay sleeping accommodations, Carlstrom Field's barracks were made of concrete block and divided into thirteen rooms. The barracks were painted a pleasing light color, more in keeping with a civilian resort than a mili-

Seen at Carlstrom Field

Below, Top Row: Administration building; palm studded walks; the swimming pool. Middle: Infirmary; mess hall.
Bottom: Barracks.

Some everyday scenes at Carlstrom Field during WW II. (ARMY AND NAVY PUBLISHING CO. INC.)

just beyond the five large hangars, two of which remain today. Here, many of the cadets took their first airplane flight and studied the theory of flight, aircraft nomenclature, navigation, and other subjects, all under the watchful eyes of their civilian flight instructors. Night flying was made challenging by the lack of field lighting; only portable lights and smudge pots were available, and there was no radio equipment. Signals between the fledgling pilot and the control tower were made by light signals of three colors, red, green and white, shown by a large hand held flashlight-type device called a "biscuit gun." Each color or series of colors had a specific meaning or instruction for the pilot. From time to time, the cadets were given check rides to determine their progress in flying the training plane. The last check ride was given by one of the two military pilots who were part of the small military contingent located at the field. One of those pilots was George Ola, who remembers that he "put on an airplane in the morning, stopped for lunch, and put it back on until the evening." Later civilian pilots would handle some of the final check rides given to the cadets.

tary barracks. Each room in the barracks, held four cadets, and had its own tiled bathroom and shower. The room was furnished with two double tier bunks, a large table for study, and matching chairs. There was also a large individual locker for each occupant. To help fight the oppressive midsummer Florida heat and humidity, the classrooms were air conditioned, and a large swimming pool was provided for off duty relaxation. Also available were tennis and basketball courts. The dining room was first class, as were the meals that were served under covered dishes, family style. No chow lines here. Additionally, there was a large canteen for refreshment and recreation.

Whatever the living conditions, work was hard, and the course was intensive. Cadets flew from a square mile grass landing area located

A British cadet is being introduced to the parachute harness while then Lt. George Ola, on extreme left looks on. On the extreme right is John Paul Riddle, the owner of Carlstrom Field.

Second Lieutenant George Ola was working for Captain Stanley Donovan as an engineering officer in September 1941 when he was promoted to First Lieutenant and assumed command of Carlstrom Field. Later, he would furnish a large part of the personnel for Dorr Field (another training field), located about ten miles away. At one time, there was a total of about 1400 trainees at both fields using a fleet of 600 Stearman PT-17's. There was one civilian instructor for every five students, and about one fourth of the cadets were American; the remainder were British. Promoted several times during his year commanding Carlstrom Field, Colonel Ola remembers the British cadets: "The Brits were fine young men, diligent in their studies. Their nation was under relentless air attack by Ger-

George and Ruth Ola.

man bombers and needed defense pilots desperately. Nevertheless, the English lads were difficult to train. Most of them had never even driven an automobile. They had no sense of speed or depth perception. This hampered their flight judgment." The two training fields had an outstanding safety record, with only one fatal accident involving an aircraft. Before that accident, about 7,900 students had flown 399,576 hours. This is the equivalent of 49,947 eight-hour days. The accident involved a United States cadet, Edward Haines, killed in March 1944.

Twenty-three British cadets died while in training at the fields run by the Southeast Training Command; however, no British cadets were killed in flight related accidents at Carlstrom Field. Today, they rest in a well main-

This photo was probably taken during an inspection tour. Leading the column is Brig. General Barton K. Yount in sunglasses, and then Captain George Ola. At the time, Gen. Yount was in charge of the Flying Training Command. (OLA)

tained American civilian cemetery just outside the town of Arcadia. There, memorial services are held each year at the British plot to honor the cadets buried so long ago. Many organizations have participated over the years at the ceremony, which was first held in 1946. Some of the groups include the Daughters of the British Empire, British veterans, former instructors, Canadian organizations in South Florida, members of the Sarasota Scottish Society, as well as the local towns' people. A plaque near the flag pole flying the Union Jack reads, "The British Plot, Oak Ridge Cemetery. Buried herein are twenty-three Royal Air Force Cadets who died while in training at U.S. flying training fields in South Florida during WW II. Erected by the Rotary Club of Arcadia, Florida, 1968." Buried in the same area, near the British Plot is John Paul Riddle, the man who played a major role in establishing the training field. He also was the civilian operator of Carlstrom and the nearby Dorr Field during World War II.

Following the end of the war with Japan in 1945, Carl-

strom Field turned out the last of its cadets, and closed later that year. The field was eventually sold to the state of Florida, and today many of the original buildings are in use by the G. Pierce Wood Memorial Hospital. Any former cadet or instructor flying over the field today would have no trouble remembering it as it was during the field's heyday in the 40s. Two of the hangars still survive in excellent condition alongside the road that circles the field, just as it did during WW II. Some barracks remain, as do other buildings including the former administration building. The administration building has been restored to its wartime appearance. In 1991, some of the former British Flying Training Schools cadets returned to Arcadia, Florida to visit their former training field and attend a reunion. Much remains of this former training field, and time has been kind to the remaining structures that were once used to help train the new pilots. If you are in the area, it is well worth a visit.

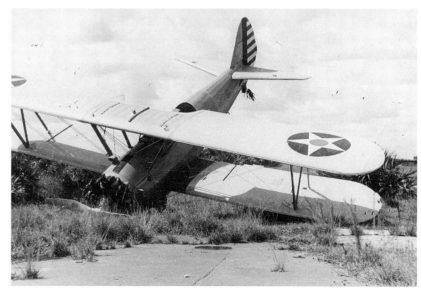

The result of a ground loop. (OLA)

The headquarters building as it appears today. It has been refurbished to its WW II configuration and is now part of the G. Pierce Wood Memorial Hospital complex.

Some of the remaining barracks as they appeared in 1998.

The British flag flies proudly over the final resting spot of the twenty-three aviation cadets who died while in training at fields run by the Southeast Training Command. The markers are in the small grove of trees just behind the flagpole.

Above: The plaque raised in 1968 by the Rotary Club of Arcadia, Florida. It informs the visitor of the historic significance of this part of the Oak Ridge Cemetery.

Left: A poignant setting for the Royal Air Force cadet graves.

Students preparing to practice their skills on one of the many Skeet ranges (USAF)

Students on the BB Range in late 1942. (USAF)

4

Gunnery Training

BUCKINGHAM ARMY AIR FIELD

By early February 1944, Florida had sixty-four Army Air Forces airfields ranging in size from single runway auxiliary strips to large complex training centers. One of the state's largest training centers was Buckingham Army Air Field. This base was located a few miles east of Fort Myers. With its three auxiliary sites (crash boat stations at Fort Myers and Marco Island, and a sub base at Naples) the base had a total area of 65,723 acres. At its peak, the field was home to 16,000 men and women and contained about 700 buildings. During its three years of operation, the base would graduate 50,000 aerial gunners from its training program. Buckingham was also the first school for flexible gunnery instructors. The field was established on July 5, 1942 and classes began on September 7, 1942.

Buckingham Army Air Field got its start when the site was purchased by a group of Fort Myers and Lee County officials, and then leased back to the government. At the time, the area was used for cattle grazing and was mostly brush, palmetto trees, and in some places, pine stumps left from a previous logging operation. The new base would create thousands of jobs, drive up property values, and bring an unprecedented business boom to the local economy. It would also have a lasting effect upon nearby Fort Myers, then a sleepy town of about 10,000, whose major source of income was tourism.

Construction of the field began in February 1942 with engineers taking soil samples. In April, work began on a canal around the runway and building area to help control the drainage problem. The canal ran around three sides of the site and emptied into the Orange River, forming the fourth side. This alone was an impressive building project. The canal was about 30 feet wide and 5 feet deep. By mid June, 1,200 men were working ten hours a day, and employment would grow to about 2,800 by mid July. Housing was scarce; some workers lived in trailers, others in shacks. One enterprising farmer converted his barn, soon named "Buckingham Palace," to house workers. Progress was rapid, and at the end of August, 483 buildings were in various stages of construction. Though the base was still under construction, there were almost 2,100 soldiers living in partially completed barracks, eating meals in temporary facilities, and using outdoor latrines. At this time, the firing ranges were also being built; however, it was clear they would not be completed for the beginning of training in September. By the middle of September, many buildings were complete, and the construction force had fallen to

Aerial view of Buckingham Army Air Field circa 1945. The rectangular shapes at the top of the photo were moving target ranges. The skeet and trap ranges were also in the same area. (PORTER)

about 1,600. The major building projects were completed by the end of November. Considerable money had been approved to camouflage the base. In anticipation of this, the builder had left the pine tree stumps in place throughout the building area; however, by January 1943 it was clear that the field would not be camouflaged, so the stumps and dead pine trees were removed to help improve the appearance of the field. When the base opened, it had three runways; later, as training demands increased, the number was increased to six. Like many other hastily built WW II training fields, most buildings were temporary, "Theater-of-Operations" type construction. They were designed to be built quickly, and were little more than wood shacks covered with tar paper or other material. Some structures were made of more permanent material, and a few remain on the site today.

Leroy Knorr was a member of the first class that graduated on October 10, 1942. He thought Buckingham was the most desolate place he had ever seen. It was very barren, with primitive roads, and poor drinking water. Called "sulphur water," it made many of his classmates sick with diarrhea. Beer was probably a good substitute because it cost 5 cents at the beer garden, at the PX, called the "Snake Ranch." Leroy also remembers being one of the first patients in the base hospital when he caught pneumonia after graduation.

Buckingham Army Air Base was never completely finished. Like many other training bases, new buildings were added, and others were changed continually throughout the war. The entire facility was constantly upgraded to make the training as effective as possible.

Training started in September when the runways were finished, but at this point, the field was no where near complete. Since there were no flexible gunnery training schools in the Army Air Corps before the outbreak of WW II, there was a desperate need for trained gunners to man the aircraft pouring from the production lines. Eventually, there would be seven gunnery training schools used by the Army Air Forces (The Air Corps was renamed the United States Army Air Forces in 1941). These schools would graduate about 297,000 officers and men. When Buckingham Field began training in September 1942, there still was no standardized gunnery training program. There were probably broad scale guidelines and objectives, but the specifics were left to the individual training schools. This was logical, because we had no experience in flexible gunnery training, and new lessons were being learned each day from aerial combat. Additionally, training equipment, including teaching aids was scarce or non existent.

A view of the former field as it is today. The runways are gone, replaced by streets for a housing development called Lehigh Acres. The ramp area is still used for flight operations. Note the extended runway on the right ramp. It is used by the Lee County Hyacinth Control District's fleet of C-47's / DC-3's for insect control spraying.
(LEE COUNTY HYACINTH CONTROL DISTRICT)

Below: A closer view of the ramp area, note the five C-47's/DC-3's.

(LEE COUNTY HYACINTH CONTROL DISTRICT)

A good indication of the training at this point is provided by Leroy Knorr. He recalls the main areas of instruction were, aircraft identification, machine gun assembly/disassembly, skeet shooting (no trap), skeet shooting from a truck, and time at the 30 cal. and 50 cal. ranges. Leroy did not like the ranges because he had to clean the guns afterward. He enjoyed skeet shooting the most, and did a lot of it. So much so, he thought his arm would fall off. He felt he was lucky he did not have to fight with a shot gun, because he could not hit anything with it. He remembers three rides in a T-6. The first was to shoot the 30 cal. at the Gulf of Mexico (this was to familiarize him with the aircraft), and the last two rides firing at a sleeve towed by another aircraft. There was no interphone in the plane, and he was held in by a belt attached to his parachute harness and to a ring bolt on the floor. He does not recall any training in the Hunt, Waller, and Jam Handy synthetic trainers. His first turret training occurred at Avon Park Army Air Field located in central Florida. When he graduated he did not receive gunners wings because there were none. Instead, he was presented with observer wings. Later, Leroy would serve with the 319th Bomb Group and fly 70 missions over North Africa and Italy.

By late 1942, Buckingham Army Air Field had developed a five week training course. The five-week course was divided into separate parts with the training day starting at 7:00 a.m. and ending with calisthenics at 6:00 p.m. Normally,

43

close order drill was the first item on the agenda, followed by range and classroom work until 5:00 p.m. The day ended with a refreshing dash of physical training in the hot Florida sun. The students also received an orientation talk by the Commanding Officer of the field, Colonel Delmar Spivey, or one of his assistants, about the dangers and rewards of aerial gunnery. Colonel Spivey also had a major role in putting together the original course plan for flexible gunnery training and helped prepare the textbooks used at Buckingham. Those schools currently in operation, and the ones that came later, drew heavily upon his work.

One of the early arrivals at the field in December 1942 was an 18 year old, away from home for the first time. Buddy Frazier was one of many who came by train to the Fort Myers station. Today the station is a refurbished historical museum that has a fine exhibit about Buckingham Army Air Field. Buddy had no basic training, and was put to work immediately on the flight line by the line sergeant; he was told he was now an airplane mechanic. His first duties were with the single engined AT-6's. The duties included gassing, pulling chocks, and holding the fire extinguishers when the engine was being started. Later he was allowed to start the engines and pre-flight the planes at the beginning of each day. He remembers the constant noise of the planes taking off and landing, and the pressure to get the planes back into the air as soon as possible. It was like working on a production line. The day started early for Buddy; his quarters were in a barracks by the flight line, and often he was awakened by the base band marching around playing the Air Force song. Later, the twin engined Lockheed AT-18 was put into use. This aircraft had a 30 cal. turret and could carry several gunner trainees.

Frazier's experience and on the job training allowed him to fly in the co-pilot seat. He operated the flaps, wheels, and whatever else the pilot wanted during the gunnery missions. Pilots were still in short supply; often civilians flew the student gunners as well as the target tow planes.

The first week of gunnery training began with classroom study of the main weapons in use on the aircraft of the day. These were the 30 caliber and 50 caliber machine guns. The student was instructed on their assembly and theory of operation, and was expected to take the guns apart and put them back together within a specified period. The 22 caliber rifle was also studied because it would be used as part of marksmanship training later in the program. The first week also included some instruction and practice using shot guns to shoot clay pigeons on the trap and skeet ranges. The purpose was to teach the feel of shooting at a moving target. During the second week, the student was introduced to the concept of relative speed and the effects of gravitational pull on the path of the bullet versus the target. Aircraft recognition was also studied along with methods used to

The diploma issued to Leroy Knorr a member of the first graduation class at Buckingham, dated October 10, 1942. The diploma is signed by Col. Delmar Spivey the base commander, and includes a picture of a P-39 Bell Airacobra. (KNORR)

Students practicing ditching procedures in the "ditching pond." The pond was put into use during the later part of 1945. Here students were taught how to exit a downed aircraft and the proper use of life rafts.   (USAF)

Below: This is what remains of the "ditching pond" as it appeared in 1996. Near here was the swimming pool which has since been removed.

at Buckingham was the skeet range, in operation by mid September 1942. In total, there were fourteen skeet ranges, all built according to the specifications of the American Skeet Association. Twelve gauge shotguns were used.

The moving base range began training at the end of September. Here the student would use the 12 gauge shotgun to fire at the clay targets while he was standing in the back of a moving truck. Each moving base range was made up of a rectangular track, about 1.5 miles long, with twenty five stations from which the clay targets were propelled into the air. The truck ran around the track at twenty five to thirty five miles per hour and the student fired at the targets as they came from the trap houses. By mid December 1942, there were about 700,000 shotgun shells fired each month, and the usage of clay pigeons was over 950,000. Even today, over fifty years later, you can still see the broken clay pigeons laying in the sand where the former ranges were located.

The third week of training saw the student shooting the 22 caliber rifle at moving targets placed on a conveyer belt. He also continued with aircraft recognition studies; ship and submarine identification was added later. A course in turret drill and maintenance was introduced using the Martin, Bendix and other power turrets. This was a particularly difficult time for the instructors at Buckingham because there

estimate range of the target. The gunner also learned how to recognize certain malfunctions and to repair them. Typically, an instructor would cause something to be wrong with the machine gun, and it was the student's responsibility to identify and fix the problem. During this week, the new gunner began practice on a moving base range. Here, he would shoot from a moving truck at clay pigeons thrown into the air.

Both trap and skeet range shooting were used to help the gunner trainee develop his skill in establishing a proper firing lead against targets appearing at different angles and altitudes. Some instruction required the student to fire from a standing position at skeet ranges while others had him firing at moving targets (clay pigeons) from a moving vehicle. The first range completed were insufficient turrets available for instructon. The school started with two different types of turrets, the Sperry and Martin upper turrets. Only ten were available at first, and this caused training problems because there were too many students for the limited number of turrets. Also, there were six different types of turrets in use at the time. As late as November, there were still serious shortages. At that time the field needed 191 turrets for training but only 140 were available.

During the fourth week, turret work continued and the new gunner was taken to the Jeep range to continue his training firing at moving targets. The range was set up so the gunner fired at a target towed by a Jeep that ran on an oval track. Some ranges used handheld guns, like those found in the waist gun positions on the B-17's and B-24's, while others had turrets just like the ones used in the bombers. The turrets were set up in the back of a truck. Distance to the target could be up to 400 yards away. During the fourth week, the blinker code was added so the gunners could signal from one bomber to another.

The fifth week marked the high point of gunnery school; this was the final week of training, and for the first time the trainee would be involved with air to air gunnery. All his training up to this point was designed to prepare him for this phase of aerial gunnery. The gunner was put into one aircraft and would fire his gun at a target sleeve towed by another. The bullet tips were marked with paint so the hits on the target sleeve could be counted once the other aircraft landed. Upon successful completion of the training program, the gunner would receive his silver gunner wings and be promoted to the rank of ser-

This is a 1945 view of the NCO Club with a masonry bridge leading to it. (USAF)

The NCO Club is gone but the bridges that led to it are still here.

geant. The next step was usually to another base for crew training or to a combat theater as a replacement member of an already existing crew. Many of the early graduates were kept on the base and became instructors.

The five-week training program was used at the time Buckingham Army Air Field opened in 1942; however, the training program constantly changed throughout the war. At first, there were few aircraft or competent instructors, and equipment was scarce or nonexistent. As a result, gunners left the field with only a minimum of the knowledge and skill needed to perform their duties. A good example of their state of training at this point is indicated by the comments of the commanding officer of nearby Page Field who received the first of Buckingham's graduates. He wrote that the gunners he received did not know their machine guns, were not proficient in turret manipulation, did not know how to fire intelligently in the air, and did not have sufficient instruction in aircraft recognition. He was also not pleased that many gunners, with just about eight weeks service, were sergeants.

Much of the training for the gunnery students used training devices attempting to simulate actual combat conditions. These were called synthetic trainers, and there were three types. The first was called the Hunt Trainer. It was a range estimation device that used scale models of airplanes, coupled with mirrors to help the student learn how to estimate the distance from his gun to the attacking aircraft. The models of the aircraft could be made to appear to move toward or away from the gunner. Also, since scale model airplanes were used, the gunner learned aircraft identification. This was a very basic trainer and was the first used at Buckingham. Seventy were ordered from the manufacturer (Reflectone Corporation) and were in broad scale use by December 1942.

The second trainer was more complex and was a significant improvement over the Hunt. The new trainer was called the Jam Handy. First used by the Navy, it was called the 3A-2, and was ordered about the same time as the location for Buckingham Field was decided. Fourteen of the new trainers were on the field by early December and were in use by the end of the month. The Jam Handy used motion picture technology to project actual combat situations on a movie screen with sound effects

An interior view of a Waller trainer. This trainer had five motion picture projectors operating simultaneously and was housed in a specially designed air-conditioned building. The trainer helped teach students the correct aim point for a moving target. (USAF)

that included engine noise. The attacking aircraft could be shown coming from several different angles at the trainee who was behind a mock machine gun. Both his skill in selecting the proper range to fire, and the aim point could be measured. If he "fired" his machine gun within proper range gunfire was heard, if not, a bell would sound. The correct aim point was projected via a ring-sight image. This could be shown

Slowly being obscured by jungle like growth; the foundations of this former Waller trainer were still visible in 1996.

continuously when the trigger was pulled or when the instructor pressed a button. Also, the gun always showed, through a spot of light on the screen where the trainee was aiming.

The most complex trainer in use at Buckingham by late 1942 was the Waller Trainer. It was a step up from the Jam Handy. The trainer required five motion picture projectors operating simultaneously, housed in an air conditioned, specially constructed building. Each of the seven Waller Trainers cost about $58,000. The Waller Trainer installations at Buckingham Field were the first in the world. Like the Jam Handy, the Waller trained the student on the correct aim point for a moving target. Four students could be trained at

the same time. Today, the remains of a Waller Trainer can still be seen deep in the brush on the former air field.

At some point, the soon-to-be gunner was treated to a flight in the altitude trainer. Early trainees at Buckingham did not receive this training probably because facilities did not exist and the need was not apparent. Buddy Frazier spent time here after being transferred to the 23rd Altitude Training Unit. While there, he lived in a tent, in an area located directly behind the base hospital. His duties included going into the pressure chamber with about 20 trainees, observing and helping them with any problems. Also observing the trainees was another person working with Buddy, and others looking through the port holes from outside the chamber. Often the trainees were frightened, and as the pressure was reduced in stages to simulate higher altitudes, some became ill with the bends, and others de-

Some building foundations which have survived over the years.

48

veloped ear problems. Later on, Buddy applied for gunnery training and flew ten combat missions in a B-29 over Japan with the 501st Bomb Group.

Another major training improvement was the use of fighter planes to give the gunner more realistic training in establishing a proper sight lead on attacking enemy aircraft. The idea was simple in concept; gunners would fire special bullets, which would disintegrate upon contact, at an armored airplane while the plane was flying toward the gunner's plane. Before the program could get underway though, many problems had to be solved. First, a unique frangible bullet that would break up upon contact had to be developed. Also, the bullet had to be fired at a reduced velocity, and this required a different powder to propel the bullet. Also, there were no available aircraft that could withstand even the low velocity impact of a frangible bullet without danger of damage to the plane. It took almost two years before these and other serious problems were sufficiently understood and initial testing could begin.

The first aircraft tested to play the role of the attacking fighter was the Douglas A-20 Havoc. This was a twin engine attack bomber with a maximum speed of 325 mph. After some

The swimming pool as it appeared in 1990.

additional aluminum armor was added to the plane, it was flown to Buckingham Army Air Field for the air to air tests. The tests occurred in late May 1944 and were highly successful, although it became clear the twin engine A-20 was not the ideal aircraft for the program. After this, the P-63 Kingcobra was selected because it met the fighter plane criteria, was available in numbers, and could be protected with the additional armor necessary to withstand the impact of the frangible bullet. The version of the plane used in the air to air firing training was called the RP-63. It had more than a ton of duralumin-alloy armor covering the parts exposed to gun fire and special instruments designed to register hits upon the plane. To help the gunner see when his bullets were hitting the plane, the propeller hub contained a light that flashed when hits were

The Fort Myers Historical Museum which was the Fort Myers train station during WW II. Thousands of soldiers went through here on the way to and from Buckingham Army Air Field. Today, the museum has an excellent display with many artifacts that help to illustrate the story of the base.

P-63, and felt they were very maneuverable and effective aircraft. Ernie recalls the armor plated RP-63 flew pursuit curves against the 30 cal. frangible bullets from the offshore waist of a B-24 flying along the Gulf Coast. Armor plated or not, he saw penetrating holes near the wing tips of the RP-63's followed by bumps as the projectile ricocheted within the wing. He just assumed that the places that really counted were better protected.

When Ernie flew mock attacks against the B-29's, he would fly a big figure eight pattern across the tail of the bomber, and attack alternately from each side. On one B-29 mission, he radioed the bomber pilot and told him he was running low on fuel and would have to make that pass his last one. The B-29 pilot responded, and said just one more pass would let him finish up with the gunners he had on board. Before Hix could answer, an authoritative voice cut in

being registered. Also, some planes had a wing light that flashed when the plane was hit. A total of 300 RP-63's were produced for the program, 200 of which were improved versions of the first model. By April 1945, the program was in place at all seven flexible gunnery schools. Prior to the use of the P-63's, another Bell aircraft, the P-39, was used to make mock attacks at student gunners while they were flying in another aircraft, often a B-17. The student used a camera rigged to a machine gun and when he "fired," the camera would record his level of accuracy against the attacking aircraft.

Ernie Hix, nicknamed "Seesaw 76," was a fighter pilot assigned to a fighter detachment in Naples Florida, and flew mock combat missions against the gunner trainees at Buckingham Army Air Field. He flew the RP-63 against the B-24's where the cadets fired back with the 30 cal. frangible bullet, and also flew a standard P-63 against the gun cameras on the B-29's. He enjoyed flying both versions of the

Near downtown Fort Myers in Centennial Park is this memorial which honors the men and women who served at Buckingham Army Air Field and Page Air Field.

The Edison Theater, one of several that were in Fort Myers during WW II. Today the former movie theater is used as an office building.

and announced, "the man said he is coming home." Ernie broke off, got a straight in approach to the runway, and as he was taxiing in, the plane's fuel warning lights were blinking. He felt good about that interruption from "home," because it may have saved him from an emergency landing due to lack of fuel.

By late 1944, the gunnery training program had undergone hundreds of changes in order to improve its effectiveness. Lessons learned in combat were added along with new technology to help make the training more realistic; however, there were still problems. One centered around training gunners for the new remote controlled defensive armament system found in the B-29. By now, Boeing's new bomber was in full production, and after extensive modifications of the engines and other aircraft systems, the plane was reaching combat units in increasing numbers. The B-29 was the first bomber with a defensive fire control program that enabled a gunner to direct the fire of several guns from a position that was isolated from the guns. It used the latest technology to compute the correct aim point, and also had the capability to transfer control of a gun from one gunner to another. This new system created a major training challenge for the personnel of Buckingham Army Air Field.

Among other things, it required different equipment and a new training program.

The most serious problem was the lack of equipment. By early October 1944, only 37 sighting stations were available when 415 were required. Also, there were no B-29's that could be used for trainers. So, the decision was made to strip turrets from 200 B-29's and divide them among the three bases training B-29 gunners Buckingham, Harlingen, and Las Vegas. Since the B-29's were not available, turrets were installed in modified B-24's. These ships were then used to train the B-29 gunners. The B-24 was probably better suited for this training; its fuselage was not pressurized like the B-29, and as a result, had more room to accommodate the trainees and their instructors. In fact, the plane could handle twice as

A partial view of the former Servicemen's Club. Here the enlisted men were invited along with relatives and dates to enjoy dancing, entertainment, and games. It was open daily from 10 A.M. to 11 P.M. Today it is used for community activities.

thousands of gunners trained by this base, or the six others located elsewhere in the United States, so it was announced that the field would be closed on September 30, 1945. The base newspaper, the *Flexigun*, reported 47,983 gunners had graduated from the school. In addition, the field had trained B-17, B-24, and B-29 co-pilots.

many students as the B-29. It took some time to get the B-24 modifications to work correctly; the first five aircraft did not arrive until mid to late October, and after arrival, they required further work before they could be used. It would be June 1945 before sufficient B-29s were available at Buckingham for training. That was just two months before the end of the war.

By late 1944, consideration was given to extending the gunnery course to twelve weeks. This was due to the need for better training. Also, by the summer of 1944, there was a surplus of gunners because combat losses had been significantly lower than anticipated; however, proper training equipment was still in short supply. The new schedule called for 673 hours of instruction with the first six weeks spent on basic gunnery instruction, and the last six on advanced training. The last twelve week course began on August 6, 1945.

Some aircraft used in the training program at Buckingham Army Air Field were the North American AT-6, (Texan) the Lockheed AT -18 (a version of the Hudson), the AT-23, (a stripped version of the Martin B-26), the RB-34 (Lockheed Ventura), the Bell P-39 Airacobra, the P-63 Kingcobra and the RP-63. Also used were the B-17, and later the B-24, and B-29.

After the war, Buckingham Army Air Field was out of a job. No longer was there a need for the

Buckingham suffered the same fate as did many other temporary training fields after they were no longer needed. Aware of the negative effect the field's closing would have on the city of Fort Myers and Lee County, efforts were made to interest the military in continued use of the field as a training facility; however, nothing resulted from these efforts. Some buildings were sold and moved off the field. The runways were destroyed and much of the land reverted to pasture for cattle. Over time, housing has been built on the land, and with the population boom in Florida, land values have increased dramatically. Today, little remains of Buckingham Army Air Field. Most of the buildings are gone, and the only reminder of the six runways is the aircraft parking ramp. Back in the jungle like growth in the old building area, you can see an occasional concrete foundation and parts of buildings used in the range areas. At this writing, the remains of the base swimming pool still exist as do some foundations for the Waller trainers; however, these reminders will be lost as the land is converted to other use. The former parking ramp is now used by the Lee County Mosquito/Hyacinth Control District as a runway and staging area for its fleet of fixed wing aircraft and helicopters.

5

Bombadier Training

SAN ANGELO ARMY AIR FIELD

The growth of the Army Air Forces prior to World War II required unprecedented numbers of bombardiers and the facilities to train them. Expansion to meet this need started with the graduation of eighteen bombardiers from Lowry Field, Texas in October 1940. These men along with others graduated in November 1940 and January 1941, were given further training to prepare them to be bombardier instructors. Prior to this, bombardier training was done locally within each bomb group. From December 1941 to February 1943, eleven bombardier schools were opened.

Texas was home to four bombardier training bases, located at: Midland (opened in February 1942), Big Spring, and San Angelo (both opened in September 1942), and Childress (February 1943). For a while, Ellington Field (Houston) also served as a bombardier training center; however, this was short lived because its facilities were required for other training needs.

San Angelo Army Air Field provides an excellent example of the build up of the bombardier training program. It opened early in the expansion of the training program and served throughout World War II as a bombardier training center. Its experience is somewhat typical of the other training schools; however, due to the

incredible demands of a nation at war, and our lack of preparation for it, the training situation was fluid and constantly changing. No two training bases did things exactly the same, especially at first. We learned from experience, and made do with what was available at the time. For example, initially there were no formal text books, few, if any, training aids, a lack of bombsights, insufficient instructors and aircraft, and worst of all, a lack of time. Only much later in the war were the resources, equipment, and facilities available to throughly train our bombardiers. Even then, there are those who would say the training could have better prepared the new bombardier for his first experience under combat conditions.

The Army Air Field located at San Angelo started out as a municipal airport to be called Carr Field; however, before construction was complete, the facility was selected as a site for a bombardier training base. The airport was to be named Carr Field to honor Robert G. Carr who at the time was a well known aviation leader and oil business man. Mr. Carr later became an officer in the Air Forces and was the Executive Officer of San Angelo Army Air Field. The field was one of two located near the town of San Angelo that had a 1940 population of about 37,000. The other field was Goodfellow Field which survives today

53

San Angelo Army Air Field as it was prior to July 1944. This picture does not include the east/west runway which was completed in July 1944.

Aerial view of Mathis Field as it is today.

was too close to the site of Goodfellow Field then under construction. The original site consisted of 670 acres and was a Federal Works Progress Administration (WPA) project. It included three runways, two of which were approximately 4500 feet by 150 feet and another around 6200 feet by 150 feet. The field's construction was well underway in January 1942 when discussions were held with the City Commission about the possibility of converting the site to an Army airfield. This was followed with a visit by the Army Air Forces Site Selection Board, in the area looking to establish several airfields in West Texas. The board found the site favorable, so on March 31, 1942, the headlines of *The San Angelo Standard-Times* announced that the new San Angelo airport would become an Army Air field. The article also talked about the housing needs for the expected influx of Army and civilian personnel, and the strain on the already over crowded school system. The announcement was no surprise to most San Angelians, because talk of the military taking over the airfield appeared in the local paper months before the announcement. More space would be needed though, so an additional 900 acres was set aside. Additional land was acquired along Lake Nasworthy for a water supply and a pumping station. Finally in May 1942, a total of over 1500 acres was leased to the government for $1.00 per year, renewable each year through June 1967. The airfield was originally named "Army Air

as Goodfellow Air Force Base. San Angelo is located in west central Texas about 200 air miles north and west of San Antonio. Today, the airport is called Mathis Field.

Construction of the field started in May 1941 to replace the old municipal airport because it

A spectacular shot of an AT-11 and two men about to leave for a night mission. Actually the shot was staged for a photo contest. Special effects lighting plus water from fire trucks helped to produce this picture which won the contest. (CARR-WEST TEXAS COLLECTION)

Forces Flying School, San Angelo No. 2 (Bombardier)." The field was also locally called Concho Air Field and was about ten miles southwest of the center of town.

With construction well under way, a temporary headquarters was set up on the third floor of the McBurnett Building in downtown San Angelo in May 1942. It was staffed by officers from Goodfellow Field who would play a major role in the field's activation. In fact, San Angelo's commanding officer during the field's construction, and until the end of the war, was Colonel George Palmer. Prior to his posting at San Angelo, he was Commanding Officer of Goodfellow Field. Military construction of the partially completed municipal field started in May 1942. By July, it was estimated that at the peak of construction the number of construction workers would exceed 3000. People from all kinds of different occupa-

tions worked on the field. These included a high school principal, farmers, a former automobile salesman, many unskilled laborers, as well as skilled craftsmen. Because of the dry ground, and the ever present wind, many workers wore dust filter masks, and eye protection. Some of the work that had to be done before the new training center was completed included the building of the water supply system. This would take some time, because it was not until mid-October that the pumping facilities at Lake Nasworthy were able to supply the field's water needs. Until then, all water for construction and use by the personnel on the field was brought in from San Angelo. The lack of items such as fire hydrants, electrical motors, urinals, showerheads, building hardware of all types, and kitchen equipment delayed construction. The field totaled 1693 acres, and by January 1944 had approximately 390 buildings of all

A partial view of the flight line with the former cantonment area in the foreground. Note the faint outline of the old base roads. Three of the hangars appear to be of WW II vintage. (BILL MCKEE, RUSTY METAL PHOTOS)

kinds and sizes. Most buildings were of the "Theater of Operations" style construction. This was essentially a one story building made of wood with a tar paper exterior, and heated by one or two coal burning stoves located in the central part of the building. The buildings had no insulation, and as a result, were very hot in the summer, and bitterly cold in winter. Other buildings such as the hospital, hangars, aircraft maintenance buildings, theater, and some training buildings were of a more substantial construction. A few of the buildings were air conditioned.

Dr. Edwin Sykes arrived at San Angelo in November 1942, just after completing his internship and being commissioned a new first lieutenant. At this time, almost all the doctors were volunteers. He remembers that the new air field had virtually no vegetation and many tar paper barracks. Later on, trees were planted. The hospital had a whitish color and was well equipped for the time. His primary duty was to practice general medicine, and be in charge of a ward in the hospital. He was a bachelor at the time, and lived in the Bachelor's Officers Quarters. His roommate was a pilot, who sometimes would take him for rides in the AT-11. On some of the flights, they would fly quite low, and had a great time during the occasional "buzz jobs" on the grazing sheep and cattle of the West Texas ranches. Sykes remembers that the view from the clear plexiglass nose of the AT-11 was spectacular.

Like most military training bases that were constructed very quickly and away from major population centers, housing availability for the families of the solders stationed at the field was a serious problem. This was aggravated by the fact that the newly opened Goodfellow Field was nearby. Both training complexes lacked sufficient housing for the families of the personnel assigned to the bases. Additionally, there were hundreds of civilian workers attracted to the well paying jobs at the air bases who had moved to the vicinity with their families, so housing of any kind was at a premium. The housing situation could have been worse if not for the help of the people of San Angelo. Unaccustomed to the sudden influx of construction workers and later military personnel, they opened up their homes and rented spare rooms and buildings that could be used for housing. The government built a 100 unit, twenty five building complex called the Rio Vista Housing Project that initially was limited to enlisted personnel and civilian workers. Also, thirty additional homes were built soon after the field opened. By August 1944, there were 863 officers and 3020 enlisted men assigned to the field. Adequate housing would continue to be a problem for the duration of the war.

Recreational facilities within the area around San Angelo included five theaters, three golf courses, a gymnasium, swimming pool, two bowling alleys, and later a U.S.O. club. The U.S.O. club (United Service Organization) was a home away from home for the solder. Here temporary quarters could be had for visiting relatives and sweethearts while they were visiting or looking for permanent housing. It was a place for meeting with friends, and had a snack bar, areas for letter writing, and making phone calls. USO's were typically staffed by friendly volunteers who wanted to make the serviceman feel at home. The emphasis was on wholesome fun and relaxation.

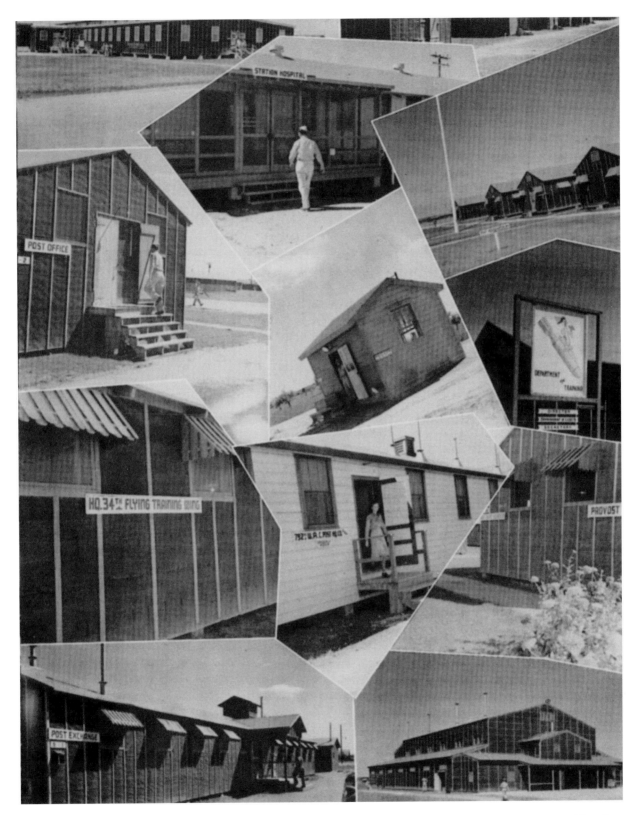

Some everyday views around San Angelo Army Air Field. The Theater of Operations type construction is evident in most of the buildings. (USAF VIA SUZANNE CAMPBELL, WEST TEXAS COLLECTION)

Three AT-11's in formation flying over the base chapels. (CARR-WEST TEXAS COLLECTION)

San Angelo. In December 1942, a Cadet Club was opened in the St. Angelus Hotel. The club was a meeting place for cadet wives and guests. Available for entertainment was a piano, juke box, a place for writing letters, ping pong table, and other games. Lake Nasworthy proved an excellent spot for a base swimming pool. It was called "The Swimming Hole" and was located on Spring Creek about one and a half mile from the center of the post. It was started in August 1943, and as time and resources allowed, improvements were made to make it more attractive for the cadets and personnel assigned to the base. By May 1944, the location had been developed into a nice outdoor park that featured a concrete dance floor, electric lights, barbecue pits, diving board, rowboats, and a juke box that required no coins.

They sponsored dances, all of which were strictly chaperoned. There were approximately 3000 U.S.O.s nationwide, and virtually all major military installations had one nearby. Agencies who sponsored the U.S.O included the YMCA, YWCA, the Jewish Welfare Board, The National Catholic Community Service, the National Travelers Aid Association, and the Salvation Army. San Angelo's first U.S.O. was located at 20 West Twohig Avenue, but later in March 1943 a new structure was opened at 19-21 East Harris Avenue. Much of the furniture and equipment of the original U.S.O. was donated by the people of

The base also published its own newspaper. The first paper was simply a mimeographed copy of about two pages. It served mostly as a bulletin of various activities around the field and was called the *Daily Bombardier*. The edition for June 30, 1944 contains the swimming schedule, along with a notice for July 4th services. Also noted, were

Yes it does snow in San Angelo! These four AT-11's sitting on the flight line prove it.

(CARR-WEST TEXAS COLLECTION)

A night shot of practice bombs being loaded aboard an AT-11. Note the dual bomb bay doors of the bomb trainer. (CARR-WEST TEXAS COLLECTION)

the Catholic Mass schedule, a Bible class notice, the time of the Protestant Service, and a car pooling request by S/Sgt. Stewart. (He was looking for two riders to and from the field). The Post Theater was showing *Double Indemnity* with Barbara Stanwyck and Fred MacMurray. Show times were 5:45 and 8:00. By 1945, the paper had turned into a professional looking weekly newspaper of several pages. It was now called the *Concho Shack*. It had pictures, news of the base, national and worldwide news, articles of interest to the soldier on the base, along with notices of events. It was much like a daily newspaper.

The first training class was 42-17 and began training in late September 1942 when the field was about 90% complete. The cadets came from pre-flight schools located at Ellington Field and Santa Ana, California. At this time, we had been in the war for about ten months, and there was an urgent need for aircraft, and trained personnel. We also lacked facilities to train the instructors, and most of all, men to crew the thousands of aircraft now being built. Once again, the

United States was paying the price for being unprepared to defend its interests. Aviators were being sent into combat with equipment and training that could have been much better had time permitted. Some paid for this lack of preparedness with their lives.

Early training at San Angelo, as well as all the other training bases, reflected the need to get men into combat quickly, but this training was hampered by the lack of resources. For example, the ground school was opened by twelve second lieutenants, who had previous teaching experience and were recent graduates of the Officer Training School at Miami Beach, Florida; however, none had any experience on the Norden Bombsight or in bombardment training. For the first class, selected trained bombardiers did the academic instruction while the twelve officers attended along with the cadets. The officers also made practice bomb drops, and went to Midland Army Air Field, when possible, to observe and learn what they could. The bombardier instructors came from the bombardier school at

Midland Army Air Field, and recent graduates from other bombardier schools.

The mechanics who were responsible for maintaining the training planes (mostly AT-11's) and the clerks who handled the paper work learned their profession "on the job" by working alongside of the few experienced men available. Some of the enlisted men who were assigned to the field had little or no prior military training, so it became the responsibility of the individual's unit to furnish the basic training. The course was four weeks long and was designed to be taken on a half day basis after the man had spent one half day in his unit performing assigned tasks. The personnel and equipment shortages prevented training in areas such as first aid and sanitation, chemical warfare drill, and range firing of the rifle and pistol. Very few of the enlisted men had ever attended a specialized army training school. At first, there was just one hangar on the field, and this was used for the most complex maintenance tasks. The rest of the maintenance was done outside on the ramp under a makeshift shelter. This meant that often repairs were made at night in bad weather with a lack of adequate lighting. This was a particularly difficult situation because training went on night and day.

The first course of instruction for the new bombardiers was just twelve weeks long, which indicated the urgent need for trained bombardiers. Later as time permitted and more trained personnel were available, the course was lengthened to eighteen, and then twenty four weeks. But at first, it was just twelve weeks and geared to move men into combat as soon as possible. In essence, it was a twelve week session devoted to the use of the Norden bombsight.

Twelve AT-11's making a formation bomb drop.

At the time, the Norden bombsight was considered secret. It was removed from the aircraft when not in use and stored in one of three combination vaults in the bombsight maintenance building. The building was fenced in and kept under armed guard twenty four hours a day. All the bombardier students were required to sign a oath of secrecy before starting their training. One of the instructors in the spring of 1945 was Warren Hasse, who received his bombardier training at Childress Army Air Field. He then flew thirty five combat missions, some as a bombardier, but most as a navigator, with the 390th Bomb Group in a B-17. After completing his combat tour, he was sent to San Angelo to be an instructor. He recalls that the proper use of the Norden bombsight demanded considerable mental and physical dexterity. As a young man, Warren had played a lot of a card game called Cribbage, which also required manual and mental dexterity. He feels this experience helped him in the classification process where he was selected for bombardier training. One of the more challenging moves required to successfully use the Norden was to operate two of its knobs located on the right side of the sight. This required simultaneous adjustment with both hands while looking through the eyepiece. To do this, the left hand had to be brought over the right hand in order to reach both turning knobs on the right side of the instrument at the same time. It was important to be able to turn the knobs smoothly and with considerable coordination in order to ensure that the bomb sight aiming point was set up correctly.

Bombardier students in class learning code. At one time, the course included 15–16 hours of work with the intent to achieve an average proficiency of taking eight words per minute.   (USAF)

An interior view of the cadet mess hall showing some of the paintings on the wall. Clearly seen is a B-17 and a B-29.   (USAF)

Most of the students who entered the course were cadets, and if they finished successfully would be commissioned 2nd lieutenants in the Air Corps Reserve; however, some classes did have students who were already commissioned officers. The training program then in use at Midland Army Air Field (Midland Texas) was used as the model for San Angelo's early program. It consisted of about thirty five hours of bombing training, actual flying missions, and about two hundred and twenty five hours of classroom work. This included a study of the theory of bombing, automatic flight control equipment, bombsight maintenance, and equip-

proximately three weeks of "combat missions." Here everything the student learned previously was put into practice in a simulated combat environment.

As stated earlier, most practice missions were flown in the AT 11. This was a twin engined, all metal aircraft built by the Beech Aircraft Corporation and used primally for bombing and navigation training. It had a wingspan of about 48 feet, was a little over 34 feet long, and powered by two Pratt & Whitney engines of 450 horsepower. Top speed was about 215 miles per hour. Most of the AT-11's used in the start up of the field were transferred from Midland Army Air Field. On board the AT-11 for the training missions was a pilot, the bombardier instructor, and two students. Most of the bomb missions were scored by one student photographing the other student's bomb drop with a motion picture camera through a special hatch in the belly of the aircraft. The scoring was based upon the number of feet the bomb hit from the center of the aiming circle (or in the case of a bomb drop on a simulated target, such as a ship or building outline, where the bomb impacted in relation to the target).

Early on, because of problems setting up the school, there was no fixed amount of practice bombs that the student was required to drop. The bombs dropped were called the M38A2. This was a 100 pound bomb filled with sand and contained a small explosive charge designed to show its impact point. Until November 1942, the enlisted personnel loaded about 600 bombs each day, but later this task was turned over to a civilian con-

There are some reminders of the field from its WW II service. These photos show the remains of building foundations.

ment. Actual bombing missions were flown with 100 pound practice bombs that were dropped at altitudes ranging from 500 to 12,000 feet. The average number of practice bombs dropped by students in the first class was about 210. Most training missions were flown with the AT-11, while a few were completed using an obsolete bomber, the Douglas B-18. The twelve week course used when the field opened was divided into four three week periods of instruction. The first was ground school (classroom work) and training on the A-2 bombing trainer. Then followed morning flying assignments, and night flying missions. Finally the course ended with ap-

One of the entrance roads that led to San Angelo Army Air Field. No longer in use today.

from the freight car. Also, the weight far exceeded the 16 pounds of the M38A2. During the course of training small quantities of 100 pound demolition bombs were dropped. Early on, the allowance per student was one; later, this was increased to two. By 1943, the only place where demolition bombs were dropped was a range called West 6. Later on, the practice of dropping live demolition bombs was probably discontinued.

When the first training class started, there were three bombing trainer buildings and two buildings used for classroom work. The bombing trainer buildings were large hangar type structures where the A-2 bomb trainer was used. This was a training device designed to give the student practice with the bombsight before he actually used the sight in the airplane. The A-2 bomb trainer was a twelve foot high steel scaffold structure mounted on wheels which could be moved electrically across the hangar floor. The top of the structure had a platform which held the student bombardier, his instructor, and a student who acted as the bomb run approach pilot. This part of the platform also had the Norden bomb sight, along with other bombardier instruments. In the lower part of the structure sat another student who operated a moveable target at which the bombardier aimed the sight. His "bomb" was a small plunger which, when released, would hit the target. The student's accuracy was evaluated based upon where the bomb hit the paper target.

tractor. The bomb was loaded with sand by the contractor and then delivered to Ordnance where a spotting charge was added prior to its being delivered to the aircraft. With the addition of newly invented automatic loading equipment, the contractor loaded 1800 bombs per day. During early 1943, the allowance of practice bombs per student fluctuated considerably due to production problems and the lack of materials.

An indication of the intensity of the training program is the fact that in the January 1943 to March 1944 period there were 448,900 M38A2 bombs dropped by the cadets of San Angelo; however, because of shortages, some Navy practice bombs had to be substituted. They were called M47A2 and were filled with water. These bombs were unsatisfactory due to leaks and dents in the bomb's casing, and their impact on the ground could not be photographed from the higher altitudes used in bombardier school. A new type of 100 pound practice bomb was received at the school in August 1943. Called M-85's, these bombs were made of reinforced concrete. They were manufactured in Pottstown, Pennsylvania by the Concrete Products of America Company and cost $7.50 each. This was considerably more expensive than the M38A2 metal practice bomb which cost $2.75. In addition to the increased expense, the concrete bomb required special handling during shipping to prevent damage, and was more difficult to unload

Louis Drake remembers instructing students with the A-2 trainer. Louis graduated San Angelo as a member of class 44-8-DR in early 1944, was commissioned a second lieutenant, and was ordered to stay on as an instructor. He thought the A-2 was an effective teaching aid for several things, one of which was helping students learn how to coordinate the Norden bombsight. He also instructed students using the Norden bombsight in the AT-11. Here, one of his challenges was to keep the student from getting flustered while using the sight; many would over correct by making constant changes in the sight.

With the exception of three mock ups of gears obtained from Wright Field in Dayton, Ohio, there were no training aids used in the early ground schools. No mocks ups of the then classified Norden bombsight, were available. To make matters more complicated, there were no textbooks. The first printed textbooks would not be issued to the students until late 1944. At the time, just one confidential handbook was on file, so the instructors had to put together their own training books and materials. In spite of these early problems, the first practice bombing mission was flown on October 21, 1942. Of the first class of one hundred and twenty students, ninety-nine graduated. A problem that plagued many of the cadets was a lack of knowledge in the areas of general mathematics, geometry, and trigonometry.

The school used 18 bombing ranges that covered more than 19,000 acres with a leased cost of about $1 per acre per year. The soil in this region was especially favorable for range construction because of the white caleche just below the surface. When brought to the surface, it allowed for a target (such as a large diameter circle) to be easily seen. Early on, the aiming circles had 100 and 200 foot radii from the target's center. Obviously the intent was to hit the center of the circle, and when this happened, the hit was called a "shack". This term was used because originally the bulls eye for the target was a wooden shack. In addition to target circles, the bombing ranges also had squares to indicate three hundred, four hundred and five hundred foot circles. Also, outlines of various shapes of ships and industrial buildings were used. In 1944, this was discontinued in order to make the scoring more accurate. The bombing ranges at San Angelo were designed by Colonel William Garland from his study of the ranges used at Midland Army Air Field.

The average distance to the targets from the air field was about 55 miles, and the average distance between targets was 15 miles. Roads had to be built to the ranges, and personnel were assigned to maintain them, and prevent the spread of grass fires sometime caused by the bombs and flares. A claims officer was kept busy investigating claims of grass fires set by the bombs on private land. By March 1944, 41 grass fire claims were processed in the amount of about $25,000. By late 1943, personnel and equipment were stationed at Eldorado and Barnhart to maintain the ranges.

The first major change in the Bombardier Course took place in July 1943; the course was lengthened to 18 weeks to include instruction in dead reckoning navigation. This caused several problems. Three groups of cadets were completing the old twelve week course, while the other groups were taking the new expanded schedule. This resulted in confusion in the course schedule and curriculum. As in the 12 week course, each instructor was assigned four students which he carried throughout the course. Typically, training was one and a half days of academics followed, by a half day in the air. To accommodate the new requirement for navigation training, the navigation and bombing missions were integrated into the same flight. For example, a flight would be scheduled so the student could navigate from San Angelo to Lubbock, Texas, then drop the bombs on the bombing range during the return trip. After Sperry Bombsight training was added in September, the training sections were reorganized and the student rotated from section to section. The sections were now specialized. By July 1943, there were about 160 instructors to instruct 493 students. This probably peaked in January 1944, when 229 instructors were responsible for 828 students.

Further changes in the training program were made in April 1944, when it was decided to stop training on the Sperry Bombsight. This step allowed more time to focus on the Norden bombsight training and was a welcome change by both students and instructors; however, it left 26 AT-11 aircraft unsuitable for Norden bombsight training because they had been equipped with the Sperry, so the planes were used for navigation training and cross country flights. The training program was changed again in October 1944 when it was increased from 18 to 24 weeks; however, there was a nationwide shortage of the M38A2 practice bombs, and this was causing problems. By this time, bombardier instructors were required to drop 20 practice bombs per month, and students could drop as many as 200. By September this number was reduced to 125. Steps were taken to substitute different bombs, one made of concrete (M85) and the other filled with water (M47A2). Neither was a satisfactory substitute. By October, there was just a six day supply of practice bombs on hand, so the Department of Training was scrambling for ways to substitute other training to make up for the lack of bombs. By January 1945, the shortage of practice bombs was over.

Some of the major changes in the new 24 week course included the extension of flying time from 120 to 150 hours. Academic hours were increased in ground school for the study of bomb racks and controls, fuzes, bombs, bombing analysis, radio aids for navigation, glide bombing, and other subjects. Added was a ten hour course in the study of the Astro-Compass. Also, more time was now available to train the soon to be Army Air Forces officers in military subjects other than bombardment. The new 24 week course started with class 44-51B. It was during this time that the student manual on bombing was received. Prior to this, much of the material was produced locally. The new manuals were written by the AAF Training Command at Fort Worth, Texas and consisted of five books titled, "Bombing," "Glide Bombing Attachment," "Allied Subjects for Bombardiers," "Navigation for Bombardiers," and "Instrument Calibration for Bombardiers."

By early 1945, the urgent need for bombardiers was over and the training had become a polished and highly effective program. Roger Myers remembers it well. He was enrolled in the bombardier school at Carlsbad Army Air Field, New Mexico during late 1944 and flew sixty two practice missions. At that time, the AT-11 carried three students. One student worked the bomb sight, one sat in the co-pilot's seat to listen for messages and watch for other aircraft, and the other was in the rear with a motion picture camera to recording the accuracy of the bomb drop. The film was developed immediately after landing so the mission could be graded. Students occasionally found ways to help each other; some bad drops were not recorded because of a "malfunctioning camera." Students who had camera

problems of this type, were required to attend a Saturday night camera class.

By March 1945, San Angelo Army Air Field was one of four training bases still teaching bombardment out of the original group of eleven bases. There were now enough bombardiers trained to meet anticipated needs, and as a result, training was more thorough. Most of the training bombs dropped were the concrete filled type. Time and experience had solved the earlier problems with this kind of practice bomb. During this time, the 1,000,000th practice bomb was dropped. The aircraft for this drop was flown by Lt. Colonel Robert Sedwick and at the bomb sight was Colonel George Palmer, Commanding Officer.

With the victory over Japan, the war ended, and so did the role which San Angelo Army Air Field had filled so well. A notice was received from Randolph Field, Texas that all bombing training would stop. Student officers and cadets were given the opportunity to remain in the postwar Air Forces and continue training. On August 18, 1945 those who chose not to remain were withdrawn from training. At this point, they were assigned other duties, and separated at the government's convenience based upon their eligibility and quotas. Most students who elected not to continue training and retention in the Air Forces expected a quick discharge from the service. This was not to be as they were assigned various other jobs around the field. The rapid decline in training activity resulted in a significant decline in the use of practice bombs. For example, in July/August there were 33,000 practice bombs dropped, while in just the previous two months, almost 103,000 bombs were used.

During this time, even though no orders had been received to close the field, things slowed down. The Aviation Cadet facilities in San Angelo, the Roof Garden and the Cadet Club were closed. Discharges from the service and transfers increased at a dramatic rate. The personnel office worked overtime handling the paperwork required to send the men to separation centers or to overseas replacement centers. At times, they worked until 10:00 p.m. in the evenings and on Saturdays. October was a particularly busy month with 1,266 men processed. The

The Santa Fe Orient Depot building as it appears today. During WW II this was the train station where many GI's came to and left the training field. It has since been restored and is now a museum.

field was probably functioning as a pre-separation center. Many men were sent here for processing until they could be moved on to the bases where they would be discharged from the service. The last class, #345, was graduated on September 12, 1945. Bombardier training stopped on September 24, 1945. The students remaining in the four classes were transferred to Midland Army Air Field to finish. For about one month, no training was done. Then in October, some training for bombardiers and pilots who desired to remain in the service was started. Also, there was some training in the AT-11 for those interested in staying in the Air Forces until 1947. In that same group were forty eight officers receiving refresher training in twin-engine aircraft. These men were former prisoners of war in Germany. By late October, and early November, there were still 116 aircraft on the ramp, most of which were AT-11's. In this group were two B-24's and two B-17's in the process of being scrapped. Some aircraft were transferred to Sioux Falls Army Air Field, Sioux Falls, South Dakota. Others were transferred to Midland Army Air Field, Midland, Texas and Goodfellow Field, which was a few miles away. Finally, the official announcement to close the field was made on November 15th. At this time, there were still about 1500 officers and 750 enlisted men

on the field. All training, both ground and flying, stopped. On Friday November 16, a meeting was held for the civilian employees in the post theater, and at that time they were given the official notice by Col. Palmer that the field would close. In November, there were 508 civilian employees at the field. This was expected to decline sharply to only the few required to maintain the field. On November 30th, the flag was lowered for the last time.

Following the war, one of the chapels was moved to Knickerbocker, Texas where it is now the Knickerbocker Catholic Church. From the time the base opened to its closing, 5,381 men were trained as bombardiers in forty one different classes. The commanding officer through the entire period was Col. George Palmer.

Today the field is named Mathis Field, and is San Angelo's municipal airport. The field is named to honor Lt. Jack Mathis, a bombardier, who received the Medal of Honor posthumously as a result of his heroic actions during a mission over Germany in March 1943. Wounded just before bomb release, he managed to crawl back to his bomb sight and release the bombs, just before dying from loss of blood and other injuries. He was a member of the 303rd Bomb Group. His brother Mark also died when his B-17 crashed into the North Sea as a result of combat damage. Mark was a bombardier who had requested assignment to the 303rd following his brother's death. Today a portrait of the two brothers hangs in the lobby of the San Angelo airport.

6

Navigator Training

HONDO ARMY AIR FIELD

The story of Hondo Army Air Field and its training of navigators actually begins with Pan American's navigation classes at the then sleepy Florida town of Coral Gables. Here, Pan American Airways System trained several hundred Army navigators starting with a twelve-week course in August 1940. Before this, some Army pilots had received navigation training at Rockwell Field in California, and others had received their training in reconnaissance squadrons and bombardment groups. In November 1940, navigator training moved into part of a two-story building at Barksdale Field, Louisiana, with twenty cadets reporting for training. This was the beginning of formalized navigator training by the Air Force, then called the Army Air Corps. The training contract with Pan American was discontinued after September 1944. At first, cadet trainees had at least four years of college mathematics, and a supposed aptitude for technical training. Even so, 20 percent failed to make the grade. Later on, the standards would be lowered; however, the failure rate remained the same. This was a function of better instructors, improved facilities, standardized course content, and the extensive use of teaching aids, including movie films. None of these improvements, however, were available for the cadets entering the navigation program in 1940.

The need for navigators in 1940 was urgent, and little time remained. A good background for this training program is given in the series of books edited by Messrs. Craven and Cate, titled *The Army Air Forces in World War II*. Volume VI.

The authors state: "Probably no other air-crew program was started with so few qualified instructors, and the shortage lasted longer than in other programs. The demands of the operational air units for navigators far exceeded the supply of qualified specialists during the first year of war; as a result, practically no experienced personnel could be spared for teaching, and reliance had to be placed upon new graduates of the navigation schools. Though not classed as instructors, pilots assigned to fly the planes used in navigation training were important for its success, and there was also a serious shortage of this type of personnel—a shortage aggravated by the policy of rotating such pilots, as well as navigator instructors, to combat organizations. . . . The training program was expanded still more rapidly in 1943, and in late 1944 the monthly number of cadets receiving navigation instruction reached a peak of more than 2,500. By V-J day more than 50,000 students had graduated from the specialized navigation schools." (Craven & Crate, pages 587 & 589).

Even with the move to Barksdale Field, fa-

An aerial view of Hondo Army Air Field probably taken soon after the field opened in 1942. (USAF)

heading necessary, allowing for the effect of wind, to follow a charted course. Pilotage requires the use of general compass headings combined with checkpoints seen from the air. Celestial navigation and radio navigation relies on the use of stars and the sun, or on radio signals from known locations on the ground to maintain a course.

To make up for the lack of trained instructors, many recent graduates were retained as teachers for succeeding classes. This action was taken to accommodate the rapidly growing number of navigator trainees who were filling the training program. Also, there was not much written curriculum, and as a result, the curriculum was prepared as the students advanced through the course. Additional subjects taught included military drill, military training and meteorology. The students received about 55 hours flying time, and those who failed the course went back to civilian life. As the training program grew, and the need for

cilities for navigator training were crowded. There was just one classroom, with such little space that the student's plotting boards would overlay the others. At first, there were only two instructors, and no aircraft were assigned to the school. Missions were flown in a variety of aircraft, none of which were suited for the training of navigators. Each plane carried two students, without an instructor. Often the student had to explain his navigation mission, or a fine point of navigation, to the pilot so the pilot could properly fly the mission. The pilots were capable, but not experienced or trained in flying navigator training missions. Classes were small, generally about twenty to twenty-five students. At the time, the course was twelve weeks long and had four parts: Dead Reckoning and Pilotage, Dead Reckoning and Elementary Radio, Radio and Elementary Celestial, and Celestial.

Dead reckoning is the computation of the speed and

Another view of the training field showing some of the cantonment area. (USAF)

improved facilities became more apparent; it was decided to close the school at Barksdale and move to new schools established at Turner Field, Georgia, Mather Field, California, and Kelly Field, San Antonio, Texas. The school at Kelly Field opened in July 1941.

With the continuing increase in navigation trainees, class size at Kelly Field increased from 20 to 120 students, and as a result the newly established school soon outgrew its facilities. At that point, the school was moved to Hondo. Complicating the situation and giving added impetus for the move was the fact that Kelly Field was also being used for advanced pilot training. By now, the flying time for the navigation student had been increased to 85 hours. Later, this would again be expanded to 95 hours.

The decision to build a new Army Air Forces training field in the area of Hondo, Texas was an easy one; land was flat, available, and was blessed with weather that was generally excellent for flying. Weather was especially important for the navigation student, because clear skies were necessary to learn the use of the octant. The nearest town, Hondo, had a 1940 population of about 2500. This was a

drawback because there would be inadequate housing availability, a lack of entertainment facilities, and not enough schools. To help ease the housing concern, the Chamber of Commerce set up an organization known as Victory Homes, Inc., in February 1942. Its purpose was to work with the Federal Housing Administration to build a large housing development; however, nothing came of it because of material shortages and the failure of the government to declare Hondo a

The runway system as it is today. The runways reflect the field's continued military service after WW II. (RUSTY'S FLYING SERVICE & LYNN POST)

One of the two remaining WW II hangars on the field today. It has since been refurbished and is now used by the Alliant Corporation for the production of unmanned aerial vehicles for the Army, Navy, and Coast Guard. Picture was taken in late 1997.

This may have been a barracks, and at the time of the photo was in the process of being refurbished. It is now used by the Hondo Art League.

Another photo of the same building, showing a WW II structure next to it that has been torn down.

"Defense Area." Adequate housing would be a problem throughout the war years.

Construction of the field began in April 1942. One of the estimated 2000 carpenters was William (Sarge) Ney whose father also worked as a carpenter on the field at the same time. Sarge remembers the site as mostly farm land with the major crops being cotton and corn. There were several homes on the field; some were demolished and at least one was bought back from the government by the former owner, and moved into Hondo where it still exists today. Sarge recalls working a 70-hour week, ten hours a day for seven straight days, and making "$1.12 and a half" per hour. (Anything over forty hours was paid at the rate of time and a half.) After taxes, Sarge received $94.67 per week; excellent wages for 1942. He recalls the union trying to organize, but with no success because the carpenters were paid union scale wages. The buildings went up fast; a typical barracks could be put up in three days by a crew of 18 men. Most of the buildings were called "Theater of Operations" and were basically wood frame structures. According to Sarge, they were made of 1' by 12' frame siding, covered by a 15 lb. felt tarpaper, attached to the frame siding by 1" by 2" wood strips. There was no interior installation, except some in the ceiling. Though they were built only as temporary structures, many buildings were still on the field in early 1998.

Sarge remembers the crews being divided into five zones; he spent most of his time in zone five building warehouses. He recalls a 40 by 110-foot warehouse with a flat roof being constructed in a week. Ottis Burrell also worked here as a carpenter's helper. His job was to run errands and make sure the carpenters were kept supplied with nails, lumber, and other materials. He also worked the seventy hour, ten hour a day week, and remembers some work, such as runway construction, going on twenty four hours a day. The construction workers came from all over, and stayed wherever they

70

The newspaper office and commercial printing plant that publishes the Hondo Anvil Herald. Originally an officers' mess hall at Hondo Army Air Field during WW II, the building was purchased by William Berger. Mr. Berger, the publisher of the Hondo Anvil Herald, moved the building into Hondo.

could find a place to put a cot. This included shacks in the back yards of homes. Ottis remembers: " Amazing what work could be done in such a short time . . . how smooth the operation went." Later on, Otis would join the Army Air Forces and spend part of his service time (twenty six months) at Hondo. When finished, the field covered about 3,661 acres, and had about 592 buildings of all types and sizes.

Bob Schultz was a young second lieutenant assigned to Hondo after training as a fighter pilot. He arrived at the field in March 1944, and was disappointed to be here, because he wanted to get into combat. Later, he would leave Hondo Army Air Field and fly B-17's. Here at Hondo, he would spend the next 13 months, first learning how to fly the AT-7 (the plane used for navigation training) and then fly students on their navigation missions. He remembers: "The base was strictly functional. I lived in a one story tar papered barracks building where two officers were assigned to each room. Our furniture was Spartan—upper and lower bunks, two desks, two chairs, a shared closet and one window. There was no air conditioning in the summer, and little heat in the winter. For obvious reasons, except for sleeping, we spent nearly all of our time at the Officer's Club, playing pool, ping pong, read-

ing, and talking. We went to movies on base."

Construction was still in progress when the field was activated on July 4, 1942. The navigation school had already opened on July 2. The early training reflected the urgent need for navigators, and the expansion pains of a massive training program begun with little experience, and few qualified personnel. The first class was 42-11N, and it graduated during August 1942 with 93 students. To put some perspective on the explosive growth of the navigation school at Hondo, a total of 652 students graduated in 1942. This compares with the August 1944 class of 619 students, the largest class. At one point, the classroom area at Hondo Army Air Field was made up of three blocks. Each block had eight

The Hondo Army Air Field service club, circa 1943. (GOUETTE VIA KUEPPERS JR.)

71

The Post Theater probably as it appeared around 1944. (GOUETTE VIA KUEPPERS JR.)

or nine school buildings and a headquarters building. The early instructors at the school were the original ones from Barksdale Field and some of the Pan American graduates who were now commissioned instructors. Over time, the class size expanded to an average of 400 students, and when the school closed in July 1945, it had graduated a total of 14,158 students.

When the school opened at Hondo the course length was fifteen weeks; however, it was soon changed to eighteen weeks with class 42-7. There was not a lot of new material taught in the expanded course, but more study time was allowed, and the flying activities were done sooner. By the time the course length was ex-

panded to eighteen weeks, much had been learned about how to most effectively teach navigation. One improvement was to establish a system in which the same ground school instructors also flew with the students; however, this was not always possible, and as a result some navigation missions flew without an instructor. At the time, about one third of the airplanes flying student missions did not have an instructor on board. An instructor was required to be aboard the aircraft for the first mission and the long "combat missions" (extended flight) which were flown late in the course. Over time, the evolution of navigator training went from, the individualistic instructor approach, with little or no training aids and little standardization, to a highly polished, centralized course, with considerable supervision, but all this took time, personnel, and experience to put into place. Eventually, even the instructors were required to fly navigation proficiency flights to maintain

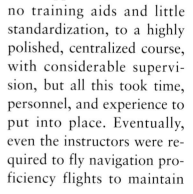

A fine interior view of the Post Theater. The seats with the white backs were reserved for officers.
(GOUETTE VIA KUEPPERS JR.)

Above: Class in session. (USAF)

their skills. Pilots were given instruction on the proper way to fly navigation training missions. One pilot directive dated 1 January 1944 noted: "The pilot and navigator must work together as a team to determine the location of the plane at all times; but the tracking and locating of the ship is the responsibility of the navigator until the safety of the ship is involved."

Bob Schultz remembers: "As a pilot, even with students and navigator instructors along, I had to be sure at all times where we were. No pilot trusted anyone else—he had to rely on his own calculations, radio communications, ground reference points, etc. An example of this was a night round trip from Hondo to Dallas and return. When we took off, there was a layer of flat stratus clouds coming in off the Gulf around 5,000', normal for early evening that time of year in Texas. Not far north there were no clouds, but when we turned around at Dallas, the overcast was almost solid all the way back and had dropped to almost ground level. By the time we reached San Antonio, all the fields there were closed with zero ceiling, and visibility. I flew the radio beam west out of San Anto-

This may have been the main entrance to the field during WW II. (USAF)

73

nio for 12 minutes, found Hondo still had a 700' ceiling and let down though a small break in the overcast. Bingo! We were right over the field. We landed well past midnight, but the students and instructors thought I was a miracle worker. Actually, I was as worried as they were."

It should be remembered that navigation students were responsible for other military subjects in addition to navigation. This additional training depended upon the need for navigators and the facilities that were available to train them. As an example, starting in 1942, navigator students were given flexible gunnery training. Sometimes this did not happen because the facilities were desperately needed to train gunners; however, by mid 1944, gunnery training was given to all navigator students prior to their entry into navigation school. By March 1944, the navigation school was running smoothly and the course of instruction was 18 weeks long. What follows is a brief review of the training at that time. (For more detail, the reader is referred to the field's official history available on microfilm from the Office of Air Force History at Maxwell Air Force Base.) The course was 18 weeks long and totaled 915 hours of instruction. The training subjects were broken into four different categories, ground school, allied training, flying, and administration. About two thirds of the time was spent in ground school, while flying missions took up about 100 hours, or 11 percent. Ground school was the heart of the program. Here the student learned the mechanics of navigation. The subjects included the four basic methods of navigation, Dead Reck-

An interior view of the AT-7 shows the aircraft empty with seats for three students. Note the drift meter next to the second seat and the headphones along the fuselage above the seats.
(GOUETTE VIA KUEPPERS JR.)

oning, Celestial, Radio, and Pilotage. During the flying part of his training, the student put theory into practice with about 85% of the flying time used to work actual navigation problems. Most flying missions were four hours long and divided into three legs. Each plane would carry three students, so each student would take turns being first, second, or third navigator on a leg.

At the time, the student was training from 7:30 in the morning until 4:30 in the afternoon, Monday through Friday with an hour off for a lunch break. Physical training ran for an hour after, followed by night study class from 8:00 until 11:30 P.M. Night study was often required for all cadets, and was mandatory for the weaker students. Saturday mornings were devoted to other training including reviews and inspections. If the student was making satisfactory progress, he had free time on Saturday after 1:00 P.M. and all day on Sunday. Sometimes weekends were used for flight time, and "free time" was often devoted to additional study and other military requirements. The course of Allied training included weather training, military subjects, code, and athletics.

While the above might indicate the course curriculum was firm and unchanging, it was not. The curriculum and methods of teaching were always under constant review by everyone involved, including instructors, their supervisors, the students, and higher headquarters. It was a fluid situation and changes were made based upon experience, new information, and the need for navigators. As an example, the course length was later expanded to twenty weeks and then due to the need for navigators, cut back to 16 weeks. The school at Hondo was also effected by the Air Forces manpower needs in other parts of the world. For example, in April 1943 Hondo had 1885 cadets with 6195 officers and enlisted men involved in their training. Just one year later, when the student load had increased to 1947 men, the number of personnel involved in their training had shrunk to 4021, a decrease of 35%.

Another example of the changing nature of the course curriculum is indicated in the official history of the base. It relates:

"No text book has ever been used at Hondo because the rapidity of developments on combat navigation would make any text out of date before it could be published. Revision of lectures is going on constantly. During the period of this installment (May–July 1944) revision has been especially marked in the material on radio navigation. The radio lectures have been entirely rewritten during the period 1 May to 1 July 1944." …

Students hard at work inside the AT-7. Here the instructor seems to be making a point with a student. (GOUETTE VIA KUEPPERS JR.)

"In general, celestial navigation has been de-emphasized, the de-emphasis coming because the development of radio aids in the combat theater, the Loran fix etc., have made celestial something which the ordinary navigator does only as an occasional auxiliary to other methods. " Probably the first textbook issued by the Air Forces was the *Air Navigation Textbook* distributed to the navigation schools around June 1944. Before that, each school supplied students with a number of materials, including maps and charts. Reference handbooks were prepared by the instructors themselves.

The most commonly used aircraft for training was the Beech AT-7, also called the C-45.

This was a twin engine aircraft with retractable gear that cruised around 200 miles per hour. It was a good plane to fly and could easily be slow rolled or looped. Typically it carried three students, an instructor, pilot and co-pilot or crew chief. In July 1944, Hondo was using 200 AT-7's in training along with other aircraft. After being checked out in the AT-7, and flying some missions as a co-pilot, Bob Schultz began flying navigator training missions as First Pilot. He remembers: "The Prescribed crew for our flights was a pilot, co-pilot, navigator-instructor, and three student navigators. The cabin had three tables on which the students did their calculations. It also had a small plexiglass dome overhead for celestial navigation. The instructor roamed among the three desks; a jump seat was in the rear for him to use when not instructing. The plane had a toilet in the back of the cabin which we called the 'Fourth Navigators Compartment.' While this was the prescribed crew, usually we flew with only a crew chief as co-pilot or with no co-pilot at all.

At first, I flew 'locals' going out to someplace two hours away and then returning to Hondo, but within a short while, I started on the real flights called 'day-nights.' This was where a pilot would fly to an airfield within a radius of 600 miles of Hondo in the afternoon, land to eat supper and refuel, then return to Hondo by night, usually getting in around midnight or later if there had been any problems. Another kind of flight was the simulated combat mission. Here, the cadet had to navigate by Dead Reckoning, fly different 'legs' (routes) and end up over a target base within certain time constraints. The pilot had to fly precise speeds and altitudes so as not to interfere with the DR calculations. A third type flight was the proficiency which permitted navigator-instructors to hone their skills flying around the country with no students on board. These were the most sought after because you could go anywhere in the U.S. for varying lengths of time so long as Operations approved. Other types of flights were taking people home for emergencies, ferrying aircraft, etc. Because I flew a lot and apparently well, I was asked to fly many proficiencies because instructors and pilots requested me. During the time I was at Hondo, I probably flew more than any other pilot. We were limited to 120 hours flying each month, so I would fly as much as I could early in the month, figuring weather problems might restrict my hours later on. This method worked. Flying a 12–13 hour day was not unusual for me."

By November 1944, after the U.S. had been at war for about three years, the teaching of navigation at Hondo Army Air Field was being handled predominantly by veterans of combat. This was causing considerable problems both for the combat returnees, and the navigation school. Many of the men now teaching had seen combat and were frustrated with the stifling atmosphere of their stateside assignment. Also, some did not wish to teach and were not particularly suited for the task. Housing was also a concern. Having survived the horrors of aerial combat, and looking forward to being reunited with their families, some were bitterly disappointed with the lack

A cadet and his navigators kit as it had probably evolved by around 1944–45. He is holding the E6B Computer and his right hand rests on the new briefcase. The small case with the handle is for the Octant which is right in front of the case.

(GOUETTE VIA KUEPPERS JR.)

of adequate housing. Aggravating the problem was the fact that many combat returnee instructors told their students that since they (the instructors) had not used some of the information taught at the school, the information was not necessary. Comments such as " well this isn't important you won't use it anyway " were common. The instructors put more emphasis into what was practical and less on the theory of navigation.

The situation was not pleasing for the administrators of the school. After having worked so hard to develop an excellent training program, they were now forced to transfer their experienced instructors to combat duty. In order to maintain quality of instruction, most of the instructors returning from combat attended a course at the Army Air Forces Instructors School (Navigation) at Ellington Field in Houston, Texas. At this point, January 1945, much of the curriculum was directed by the Instructors School at Ellington Field. This compares with the early days at Hondo when the development of the instruction depended upon the initiative and ingenuity of the personnel running the school. By now, the course had been expanded from 18 to 20 weeks.

Over time, adjustments were made, and while the quality of instruction suffered, it became apparent that the combat veterans now teaching brought a dual advantage to their new job. They were respected by their students and imparted much of their combat experience to the cadets in the instruction of navigation; however, the replacement of instructors and other key personnel continued to create problems with the quality of teaching. Sometimes this meant that on the job training was required, because the school did not have the sufficient lead time necessary to prepare for the transfer of instructors. Also, supervision became less effective, and some instructors did less than their best because of post combat let down. In addition, the transfer and replacement of personnel often gave the impression that the job was temporary.

Jack Taylor flew 35 combat missions as a navigator in a B-17 after graduating from the navigation school at Selman Field in Monroe, Louisiana in April 1944. He remembers the navigation course being 16 weeks long, with the last half devoted to celestial navigation. He became quite proficient with celestial navigation but used it just once during his combat tour, and that was to navigate his aircraft on the flight from the United States (Newfoundland) to England. After that, it was mostly Dead Reckoning, and Pilotage. In general, he feels the instructors at Selman Field were excellent. At that time, there were no combat returnees being used as instructors at Selman Field, and a college degree was not required for navigation training; however, Jack had taken some math courses in his year and a half of college, and was comfortable with the math required to navigate. There was still an upper and lower class, and hazing was in vogue, but, by the time he moved to the upper class, the practice of hazing was discontinued. He still recalls the upperclassman standing in his face and demanding that "he wipe the smile from his face the Air Forces way—up not down."

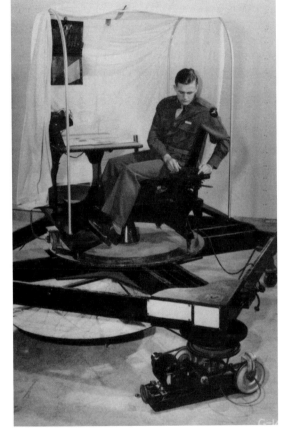

This could be a photo of the "Navi-Trainer." It appears as though it is designed to simulate travel over a map which is located on the floor.
(GOUETTE VIA KUEPPERS JR.)

Jack remembers using a method of navigation not taught at the school, but still very effective for getting home from a combat mission, especially when the aircraft was damaged. It was called flak navigation. The navigator could find his way using the known areas of heavy flack, generally found around large cities, or important targets, to steer a course back to England and safety. The trick was to avoid the flack and simply compare its location with known areas of heavy flack. Then fly from concentration to concentration toward home.

With the end of the war in Europe (May 1945), Hondo Army Air Field, underwent several changes in its mission. For a while, the school continued to train navigators. Later, it became the Air Forces Flight Engineers school for the B-29. Hondo was also the site of a B-24 pilot transition school, and had a brief fling with teaching newly minted bombardiers the science of navigation. Meanwhile, the navigation course was extended from twenty to twenty-four weeks during May 1945. The new subjects included, radar indoctrination, over water flight, and cruise control. Over water flight was a sudden addition to the training program which caused confusion in the curriculum.

The training of bombardiers to be navigators is a rather interesting side note in the history of Hondo Air Field. Apparently the bombardiers were not too happy to be here. After having undergone a long and intensive course in aerial bombardment (at another training base) they were now in a somewhat remote area and faced with the prospect of taking another (perhaps more difficult) course. It was thirteen weeks long. The newly commissioned bombardiers had hoped for flying duties but were now faced with the prospect of yet another school. By now, the new Second Lieutenants had probably had their fill of Army schooling. The history notes that "Military bearing and discipline have continued to be a problem among the bombardiers." . . . "there remained a large proportion among them who had little or no interest in navigation and whose attitude remained apathetic, bored and often uncooperative."

The B-29 Flight Engineer training program was a major training effort at Hondo. The first class started in June 1945, and the last class graduated in November. Robert D. Thompson writes in his history of Hondo Air Field, *We'll Find the Way*, that 2940 students graduated the school. The school was transferred from Lowery Field, Colorado and used a different aircraft than those at Hondo for navigation training; however, there were not enough B-29's available to use for the new training, so a specially modified B-24 (B-24J) was used in its place. While the B-29 school was starting up, the navigator school was being phased out. The last class graduated in July 1945.

This was a particularly unsettling time at the school for many reasons, some of which were the change in course length in the navigators school, the continued loss of experienced personnel through transfers and discharges, the changes required in gearing up for a new instruction course, and the closing of another. In short,

A trainer that probably appeared later in the training program and may have been used to help the cadets learn the use of the octant for shooting "sunlines" or stars. (GOUETTE VIA KUEPPERS JR.)

a totally new school was about to begin. This required different aircraft, pilot training on the aircraft, hundreds of trained mechanics, and skilled instructors, along with different teaching aids, and manuals. To help ease the maintenance problem, 570 maintenance men were transferred from Courtland Army Air Field, Courtland, Alabama to Hondo during June.

With the end of the war, students were asked if they wanted to remain in the post war Air Forces. Those who elected to remain continued with the Flight Engineer program, and the others who wanted out were dropped from the school, and assigned general duties on the field. Even though the war had ended, and the last class graduated in November 1945, Hondo was still a busy place. As an example, in September and October there were 8812 landings and takeoffs from the field's four runways. In October, the field had 81 aircraft and at the end of the month there were still 4184 military personnel assigned to the base.

Orders to shut down Hondo Army Air Field were received on November 20, 1945, to become effective on December 31. Slowly, the base was closed down. The Flight Engineer school had been transferred back to Lowery Field in early November, and by the 13th of December 64 excess aircraft had been ferried to temporary storage. By now, there were just two B-25's left. The field was quiet and was beginning to look like a ghost town. November and December were particularly difficult months for those still stationed here, because places to go for recreation were being gradually phased out. This included the bowling alley, li-

Evelyn Herrmann standing next to a P-51 in front of the Flightline Cafe. The building was a barracks in WW II and used as a pilot ready room in the Korean War. The building was moved to its present location. (HERRMANN)

brary, Postal Exchanges, Officers Club and the movie theater. During the first week of December the post gym was turned into a warehouse to help store base material, and the hospital was closed on December 1. Many of the officers who were unassigned or awaiting transfer were required to do jobs normally handled by the enlisted personnel. For example, three officers were assigned to the chemical warfare department to help with the packing and crating of gas masks for shipment to a depot. This was necessary because people of all ranks were being discharged or transferred and there was no one else left.

During the three years of the field's service during WW II it had six different Commanding Officers. They were: Col. Linus D. Frederick, Lt. Col. G. B. Dany, Col. Charles H. Dowman, Col. Robert B. Davenport, Col. William L. Kimball, and Col. James A. Ronin. Lt. Col. Dany served the longest period, from November 1942 to November 1944. His contribution was sig-

nificant; he played a key role in the establishment of the school and was instrumental in making it the effective training program that it was.

Hondo Army Air Field's role in the training of Air Force personnel did not end with its closing in 1945. Over the years, it has served in several capacities for the Air Force and continues to the present day. Today, it is the site of one of the Air Force's two Flight Screening Centers. There are 52 Slingsby Fireflys here flown by the 3rd Flying Training Squadron. The planes are used to evaluate a student's potential for further pilot training, but are temporarily grounded with engine problems. The former training field is also a growing industrial park owned by the city of Hondo. Visitors to the field should be sure to stop by the Flight Line Cafe. Here, visitors can have an excellent meal, meet Evelyn Herrmann who is very knowledgeable about the field's history, and see some of the field's history on display in the cafe.

Soldiers outside the barracks preparing for morning roll call. This photo may have been taken on a Saturday during 1942. (DUSSLER)

Soldiers outside the barracks after a Saturday "GI Party." Bunks were removed from the barracks while the barracks was cleaned, 1943. (DUSSLER)

7

Pumpkins and Atom Bombs

Wendover Field probably had many un official names. One of the more de scriptive was "Leftover Field", a name given it by Bob Hope when he was on a USO tour visiting the airfield. Bing Crosby also visited here and called the nearby town, "Tobacco Road with slot machines." The town was named Wendover, and at the time of the airfield's construction it had one paved road and a population of about 100 people. Within a few short years, during the early to mid 1940s, this isolated, unknown field would become the world's largest military reserve. It also would help train and launch the crew that would drop the world's first atom bomb. Today, part of this field, located about one half mile south of the city of Wendover, Utah, is listed on the National Register of Historic Places.

The field's history begins in 1940, when the Air Corps was looking for bombing and gunnery ranges. The area near the town of Wendover seemed to fit these needs. The land was virtually uninhabited, had generally excellent flying weather, and the nearest large city (Salt Lake City) was 100 miles away. The area, part of the huge, wide-open expanse of the Great Salt Lake region, was secluded and lonely. Though isolated, the town was served by the Western Pacific Railroad,

and many of its citizens were employees of the railroad. Other important factors in locating the base here included the Army's intention to convert Fort Douglas (an infantry post at Salt Lake City) into an Air Corps facility, and use Salt Lake's airport as a field for heavy bombers. But this didn't happen because of the danger of keeping large quantities of high explosives near the city. Prior to this, explosives were stored at Salt Lake's airport and practice bombing runs were made over the Salt Lake Desert by planes stationed at the airport, so it made sense to eventually move the planes and armaments out to the more remote site.

There were several stages in the building of the airfield at Wendover; the first part started in November 1940 with a gravel runway system and just a few buildings. By the end of 1941, the field had been expanded with additional buildings and paved runways. This was the condition of the field when the first military personnel, about twelve men, arrived in August 1941. In this group of men was a gunnery and bombing detachment. Facilities were spartan, with just a few barracks, officer's quarters, and a mess hall. There were also some warehouses, a theater, a medical facility, and a few other buildings. The field was officially opened on July 29, 1941; however, it was not until March 1942 that the

Wendover Air Force Base circa 1956. The former Technical Site is clearly shown as are the bomb loading pits. Note the size of the ramp in relation to the cantonment area. (USAF)

base was officially recognized as a separate air base. Prior to that, it was considered part of Fort Douglas. A major expansion program began in 1942 and a total of 668 buildings were constructed, mostly the Theater of Operations type. These were temporary wood frame buildings designed to be built with the least expenditure of time and material. Included in the expansion program was a 300-bed hospital, gymnasium, library, chapel, bowling alley, swimming pool and housing units for married officers and civilians. The largest part of this building project was completed at the end of 1943. At the time, there was a total of about 19,500 military personnel and civilians on the base. By now, Wendover Field had 3,500,000 acres and was the world's largest military reservation.

Training began in April 1942, with very few training facilities and primitive living conditions.

The base had less than 12 buildings to house the first bomb group that arrived for training. Conditions were so basic that the same room was used as a headquarters for the bomb group and the individual squadrons. Fifty to sixty men worked just inches apart at a series of small tables that were arranged in a "U" shape. The tables were just boards put over carpenters' horses, and the filing cabinets were used cardboard boxes. Sometimes, the men had to do their own construction work. For example, they built their own USO center with the help of people living in the towns around the base. The center was constructed in one day, and was in use the same night. Range facilities were austere but were expanded over time. This included the building of life-sized targets of battleships, the installation of night lighting, and the construction of rifle, skeet, and machine gun ranges into the hills

about four miles from the base, but not all these facilities were available for the 306th Bombardment Group, the first group to train here.

Wendover's mission was to train heavy bomb groups. At the time, heavy bomb groups were using either the B-17 or the B-24. As with the other training programs throughout the Air Forces, the training of the bomb groups was constantly being changed and modified. Originally we had little experience, few qualified personnel, and precious little equipment. Over time, this changed, and as it did, so did the training programs. At first (March 1942) heavy bomber training was a two-phase program, with each phase being six weeks long. Later, the training was changed to a three-phase program,

and each stage lasted four weeks. Wendover would do the second phase training. The first bombardment group to train at Wendover was the 306th when it arrived at the field in April 1942 for training with the B-17. Later on, B-24 groups would train at Wendover. In total, 21 bomb groups trained at Wendover.

During 1944, the system that required different bases for different parts of training was changed. Now, all phases of training would be given at the same Operational Training Unit (OTU) station. Wendover continued its group training under the new system. This training stressed the importance of teamwork and included high altitude formation flying, long range navigation, target identification, and simulated combat missions.

For a short time, beginning in May 1944, the field trained fighter groups; however, this was abruptly canceled in September 1944. That month, B-29's arrived on the field, as part of an operation code named "Sil-

A look at the ramp area of the air base. Shown are six hangars, and in the upper right-hand corner are the barracks and part of the hospital complex. The last hangar is the "Enola Gay" hangar which was built for the B-29's of the 509th Composite Group. (DAVE)

Another view of the hangars along the flight line. The three major groups of buildings behind the flight line and in the center of the photo are the remains of the former hospital complex and barracks. The dry air along with the work of interested people have helped to keep the buildings in a remarkable state of preservation.

ver Plate." They would begin preparation for the dropping of the world's first atom bomb in August 1945. This operation and everything connected with it required utmost secrecy. The base itself was given the code name "Kingman," and the activity to assemble, modify and flight test prototype bombs was code named "Project W-47." The only flying unit on the field was the 393rd Bombardment Squadron, which would later become part of the 509th Composite Group.

As part of the buildup of the 509th Composite Group, about 800 people stationed at the field, were transferred into the group and began training. Some of the other units transferred were the 390th Air Service Group, the 320 Troop Carrier Squadron, (the "Green Hornet Airlines") the 1395th Military Police Company, and later the 1st Ordnance Squadron. In addition, qualified personnel throughout the military were filtered into the group. Only the commander of the group, Colonel Paul W. Tibbets, had full knowledge of its mission. Security was intense, and to help maintain it 400 FBI agents were involved. Personnel were instructed to talk with no one about their activities, not even among themselves. Those who did were immediately transferred from Wendover to other assignments, some as far away as Alaska. Most of the 509th Composite Group's training (which included individual as well as crew training) was done at Wendover. Crews were trained to drop one bomb

Some of the barracks as seen circa 1942. The plain, single story building is an example of "Theater of Operations" construction, while the two story buildings represent "Mobilization" type construction. (DUSSLER)

This was probably a mess hall and has changed very little from its appearance during WW II.

A building located within the hospital complex. This was probably used as living quarters for personnel assigned to the base hospital.

A 1941 view of the first PX at Wendover Army Air Base.
(DUSSLER)

Two views of the Enola Gay hangar built for the B-29's stationed here late in the war. It was used by the 509th Composite Group commanded by Col. Paul W. Tibbets.

which now contained high explosives, over Japan while awaiting the atom bomb.

The story of Project W-47 is not well known, and somewhat controversial The story begins in the ordnance area which was located on the south side of Wendover Field far away from the main body of the other base buildings. The two areas were separated by the base runway system and joined by dirt and/or cinder roads. The ordnance area consisted of several wooden and metal frame buildings, with no running water and no inside plumbing. Also located within the area were some igloos for the storage of explosives. Later on, additional buildings were constructed which became explosive assembly buildings. Outside the ordnance area were the two sets of pits used to load the oversize bombs into the specially modified B-29's. One set of pits was located on the northwest part of the aircraft parking ramp and the other set was found on the taxi strip on the west side of the field. The area was so isolated that the men working at the site were transported back to the main base for meals. This was the situation in May 1945 when Captain James L. Rowe became project officer in the area now being called the technical area.

At the time, little was known about the flight characteristics of the prototype atom bomb designs and how the fusing mechanism would work. The prototype bombs were assembled at the technical site by men, most of whom had little or no technical experience. So secret was this work that Captain Rowe had virtually no

with a high degree of precision, and to execute a sharp turn after dropping it in order to avoid the effects of the nuclear blast. These practice bombs were called "pumpkins" because some, if not all, were painted orange; also, one of the two types being tested had a round shape. After completing the training at Wendover, the 509th went to Tinian Island in the Marianas. From here, the group continued to drop the pumpkins,

The author's daughter standing in front of one of the smaller hangars on the flight line at Wendover Army Air Field.

A view from the ramp of some of the hangars along the flight line. The smaller buildings between the hangars may have been operations buildings.

Today's Operations building with a WW II hangar on one side. The building contains the airport manager's office and a wonderfully detailed diorama of the field as it was in 1945.

A former base chapel as it was in 1996.

A 1942 view of an early building and the desolate, barren space surrounding the air base. (DUSSLER)

The fire station located on the flight line, it is still used as a fire station. The building was also used for bombardier training.

88

contact with his military superiors, except a monthly visit from a representative of the Joint Chiefs of Staff. Captain Rowe's group worked 24 hours a day, six days a week helping perfect the design of the prototype bombs, later called Fat Man and Little Boy. Much of the technical work was done outside the site but the prototype bombs were assembled there. Once assembled they were loaded into specially modified B-29's and then dropped over Wendover's bombing ranges, and perhaps elsewhere. The flight characteristics of the bomb would be noted, analyzed at a different location by scientists, and changes in design ordered. It is at this point that the story of Project W-47 becomes a bit controversial. According to Captain Rowe, the final assembly of the two atom bombs dropped over Japan took place at Wendover Field. A full and fascinating story of this part of Wendover's history, can be found in *Project W-47*, by James L. Rowe, published in 1978 by Ja A Ro Publishing, Livermore, California.

The training of B-29 aircrews and the testing of prototype atom bombs was the last major contribution of Wendover Field during WW II. After the end of the war with Japan, some crew training continued, but at a reduced level. For a while, B-29's were stored here. Among other things, some work was done with the Air Material Command's weapons development program that included the testing and development of missiles. Some of these missiles were German V-2 rockets that had been confiscated and then sent to Wendover. For a short time, the Strategic Air Command used the field and its ranges for training. In 1948, the base was deactivated and then declared surplus in 1949. Later in 1955, while the field was being used by

Two views of the former airmen's barracks, each building housed 24 men. Showers and restroom facilities were in another building built for that purpose and shared by men from several barracks.

SAC and the Ninth Air Force, work was done to update some of the facilities. The base was again deactivated in 1957, and the next month renamed Wendover Air Force Auxiliary Field. It was used from time to time by various Air Force units for gunnery practice, summer encampments, and other uses. In 1960, the field was placed in caretaker status under the management of Hill Air Force Base which is located near Salt Lake City, Utah. Wendover Field was again re-

This was a Link trainer building where pilots practiced their instrument flying skills. Behind the building can be seen part of the Enola Gay hangar.

plex and hangars. Some acres including the radar site were retained by the military.

Today, the field is an active airport that still retains much of its WW II history. One of the WW II hangars still remaining is called the "Enola Gay Hangar" because it was built to accommodate the B-29's of the 509th Composite Group. Numerous buildings remain from this period including the first headquarters (building 211), the enlisted men's barracks, a few buildings from the base hospital, a Link trainer building, and several other structures. The buildings are in generally good condition, due to the dry climate and the efforts of concerned citizens. There are several attractive informational signs placed at various locations around the former base. These help the visitor better understand the role the field played toward speeding the end of WWII. Also, inside the airport manager's office is an excellent diorama of the field as it appeared

activated in 1961 with only a fire protection group of 15 men stationed on the base. Some of the buildings were removed, and by 1962 only 128 of the original 668 buildings remained. The base was again declared surplus. The government was willing to sell the base and retain the bombing ranges and radar site. At this time, the City of Wendover, now with a population of 800, sought to interest commercial firms in the base; however, this was not successful, and a small crew of civilian firefighters remained until 1977. Meanwhile, various Air Force units used the facilities from time to time on a temporary basis. The field was again declared surplus in 1972. Earlier the ranges had been incorporated into the Hill Air Force Base range complex. In July 1975, the base was officially listed on the National Register of Historic Places. In 1977, the government deeded much of the old field to the City of Wendover. This included the runways, the former hospital com-

A distant view looking toward the flight line of some buildings remaining on the former base.

SQUADRON ADMINISTRATION

Fire Station/Link Trainer buildings. Directly east of the 847th Squadron alert building is the base fire station and bomb training building (#1800). This building continues its fire fighting role for the airport. East and north of the fire station are various smaller buildings which originally housed the Link Trainer (building #1804), a boiler house (building #1807), and base engineering (building #1808). Just eastward from the fire station is building #1809 which housed the bomb site storage, communications and transmitter facilities. Imagine the security surrounding the bomb sighting equipment – which eager adversaries would have highly prized. This equipment was the most advanced system in the world and assured greater bombing successes in each mission.

LINK TRAINER BUILDING #1804   BASE ENGINEERING #1808
FIRE STATION/BOMB TRAINING #1800   BOILER HOUSE BUILDING #1807

Historic Tour Marker 9

One of the many informational signs posted around the former airbase that inform the visitor about the buildings and some of the base history.

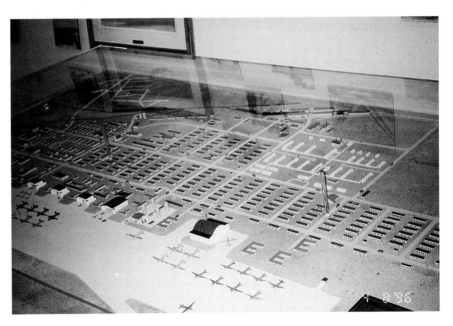

The Wendover Army Air Field diorama that shows how the field looked during 1945. Located in the Operations building, it is a must see for any visitor.

during the time when the 509th Bombardment Group was here. The airport manager and life long resident, Chris Melville is very knowledge-able of the field's past, and has played an impor-tant role in the efforts to preserve the history of Wendover Field. Still, much remains to be done to help insure this part of our national heritage is here for future generations. Unfortunately, lack of funding has been and continues to be, a seri-ous drawback to any significant restoration and preservation efforts. Unless help comes in the near future, continuing building deterioration, and lack of public support, will cause this part of our his-tory to be lost forever.

8
Pilot Training and Aluminum Ingots

The history of Walnut Ridge Army Air Field is fascinating. The field, originally intended to be an advanced glider pilot school, was used instead as a basic pilot school, and then turned over to the Navy. When the war ended, and training had ceased, the field was used as a site to at first store, and later scrap thousands of aircraft, some fresh off the assembly lines. In effect, the field had gone full circle — from training pilots to fly the planes that later would be turned into scrap.

The story of Walnut Ridge Army Air Field begins in Dyersburg, Tennessee where early plans had been made to build a training field; however, the plans changed when it was determined that construction of the field there was not practical. At the time, it was felt that site preparation would be too costly. So, the Project Officer for the proposed field at Dyersburg, Colonel John Guillett, and his construction engineer Harry Hurley, were sent to Walnut Ridge, Arkansas to build the field about three miles northeast of Walnut Ridge.

There were three other Army Air Forces training bases located within about a 75 mile radius of Walnut Ridge. One was an advanced twin engined training base at Blytheville, Arkansas about 60 miles southeast of Walnut Ridge, Blytheville Army Air Field. The other two bases were both basic training bases, one was near Malden, Missouri (Malden Army Air Field), and the other was Newport Army Air Field, about six miles outside of Newport, Arkansas. Apparently, the site problems that prompted the build-

In addition to bombers, fighters were also scrapped at Walnut Ridge. Here are seen P-40's with their engines removed, stacked on their noses. Most of the aircraft had the national insignia painted over.

(U.S. AIR FORCE MUSEUM)

An aerial view of Walnut Ridge Army Air Field as it was just after the base opened in 1942. Note what appears to be another runway at the top of the photo. (USAF VIA ROBERTA WILLIAMS)

ing of the base at Walnut Ridge instead of Dyersburg, Tennessee were solved because a major training base was built on the site in Dyersburg, Tennessee. This became Dyersburg Army Air Field.

At the time of the base's construction, Walnut Ridge was a small rural community of about 2000 people, located in the northeast corner of Arkansas. Farming was the major occupation with crops that included cotton, corn, and hay. Some of the other commercial interests were a few sawmills for the cutting of timber and cotton gins for the processing of the cotton grown in the area. The construction of the field here was a blessing in some ways because it changed, almost overnight, a poor rural community where jobs were scarce and pay low, into an economic boom

town. People, who had worked for as little as fifty cents a day, could now earn as much as thirty-five dollars a week. Walnut Ridge would never be the same.

Construction of the new airfield started on June 20, 1942, after considerable work on the selection of the site was completed. The area was studied by soil technicians and engineers, the availability of housing and transportation was analyzed, and facilities for schools and recreation were reviewed. Then steps were taken to purchase the land and notify those people living on it that their lives were about to be disrupted forever.

Dr. H. E. Williams founder of Williams Baptist College, which is now located on part of the former training field, remembers that about 150 to 200 people were forced to move from the land.

The former air base as it appeared in 1996. The two remaining WW II hangars are visible, one at the far end of the ramp, the other is the structure on the ramp across from runway 17. (ROBERTA WILLIAMS)

If they could not move their homes within thirty days, the houses were burned. This was particularly sad because many of the homes were well kept, and occupied by tenant farmers. When construction began the homes, barns, other buildings, and a rural school would be moved or destroyed so the 3,049 acres could be turned into a first rate flying school.

As mentioned, the flood of construction workers and others attracted to the site, had an immediate impact upon the area around Walnut Ridge. Because of its rural location and distance from a major city, there were very limited facilities for housing the thousands of additional workers and their families who came to the new training center. To help alleviate the problem, a survey was taken in the small towns of Walnut Ridge and Pocahontas to determine the amount of housing available. In Pocahontas, the Boy Scouts helped with the survey. Also, a newspaper ad was run in the Walnut Ridge paper, the *Times Dispatch* announcing that living quarters were needed. About a hundred rooms were found to be available in Walnut Ridge after the first thirty days of the campaign. In Pocahontas, about 15 miles from Walnut Ridge, there were about 250 rooms and about 200 houses or apartments with available room. Some of the home owners moved into their basements or garages in order to create room for the military personnel. Eventually, additional housing was built on the field and about twenty-five additional homes were built in Walnut Ridge; however, adequate housing would remain a problem.

Soon after construction started, a temporary field headquarters was established in August 1942 in the Mize Motor Building in Walnut Ridge. Later when a building became available, the headquarters was moved to the field. Because of the lack of living facilities, many of the enlisted men who were sent to the field during its construction lived at a former Civilian Conser-

Two views of the ramp and cantonment area taken in November 1942. Both photos were taken on the same day.

(USAF VIA ROBERTA WILLIAMS)

vation Corps camp near the small town of Pocahontas. The first commanding officer was Colonel John F. Guillett who was with the airfield from the start. Colonel Guillett helped to select the site, supervised its construction, and selected key personnel.

An interesting note is that as late as September 1942, it was intended that the field be used as an Advanced Glider Training base. Early

This is the sub-depot hangar and the location near where the smelter was located just after WW II.

The only other WW II hangar remaining on the former training base.
At the time of the photo it was being used by a company that makes portable buildings.

preparations to use the field for glider training included requests for instructors, gliders, study material, and other items; however, by the end of the month, the confusion was ended when 102 aviation cadets, three student officers from the primary school at Decatur, Alabama and 20 cadets from the primary school at Camden, Arkansas were ordered to report to Walnut Ridge Army Air Field for basic pilot training. The first training class was Class 43-B, which began training on October 10, 1942 with 59 instructors.

The story of the start up of training at Walnut Ridge is typical of so many other temporary training fields rushed to completion in the early days of World War II. Conditions here were primitive. The auxiliary fields were not completed, and there was just one usable runway. Since the ramp would not be complete until November, the airplanes were parked and maintained out in the open by the runway. Conditions were made worse by the poor weather in December, and the size of the next class (43-C), which had 308 students. Everyone suffered from the need to turn out pilots as soon as possible. The students were affected by the poor living conditions in the Theater of Operations type barracks, damp and cold in the winter, and hot and dusty in the summer. The field was as yet not sodded and the roads and walkways were not complete. So mud and water collected after a rain storm, and dust was everywhere when the ground was dry. These conditions, combined with the frequently unappetizing food prepared by the new mess hall personnel, often resulted in colds and other health problems.

Also, at this time, there was little in the way of recreation facilities, either on the base on in the nearby towns, and as a result, the morale of the people stationed at the new airfield was not good. At first, the emphasis was on building the facilities needed for training, then as time and resources permitted, the priority was shifted to improving living conditions. Some of the new structures added to the airfield included civilian worker dormitories, a recreation building, and a mess hall, all of which were built by April 1943, about seven months after training started. One of the first major recreation facilities built at the field was the post theater, which opened in late 1942, with a seating capacity for 600 people. The theater had several uses, including a classroom, a meeting hall, and a place for USO shows and movies.

These buildings, now on the campus of Williams Baptist College, may have been enlisted men's family quarters. One is in obvious need of repair and by now may have been torn down.

The movies shown were generally the latest, and were normally screened on the base before the civilian theaters in the nearby towns had them. The movies were a popular form of entertainment, and by 1943, they were shown seven days a week, with two showings per evening, and a matinee on Sunday. Normally, the movies were changed every two days. Another popular form of recreation were the dances for the enlisted men. Because there were no other facilities available, the dances were first held on Saturday nights in the buildings used by the post engineers. Another improvement that helped morale was the enlisted men's service club which opened in July 1943. The club had a lounge, some game rooms, a library, and a cafeteria. The non-commissioned Officer's Club was in use by November 1943, and featured a dance floor, a compete bar, and other amenities. It was about this time that the station newspaper *The WRAAF Pilot* began publication. Other improvements included an expanded library, bowling alley, a swimming pool (opened in August 1943) and a U.S.O. club in Walnut Ridge. These plus an increase in availability of family living quarters, and a much enlarged Post Exchange significantly helped raise the morale of the people assigned to this remote base.

These improvements, however, were all in the future, and when the first of the army personnel

This building was moved from its original location at Walnut Ridge Army Air Field to it present location. Rented for many years it was derelict at the time of the author's visit.

Said to be the former officer's club swimming pool, it was being used by a company that makes fire fighting equipment.

Quonset hut type buildings that are said to have been built during the brief period when the Navy used the former Army Air Force training field.

reported to the base, they were greeted with drab temporary-type buildings. There was construction and mud everywhere, few amenities, and not much prospect for immediate improvement. Since at this time, basic training was a nine-week course, the student could look forward to leaving Walnut Ridge and moving to another station for the next phase of training; however, those assigned to the field in a support or teaching capacity, had no such pleasant expectations. So they put up with it, and made the efforts necessary to turn this raw new training center into a first class flying school.

The first Director of Training was Major L. J. Purdue, who arrived on the field in late September 1942 and would serve in this capacity until September 1943. His work was made especially difficult because the field's mission was changed just prior to its opening. Added to this were the normal problems associated with the start up of a new training field in 1942. At this point, the nation was still recovering from the shock of Pearl Harbor and was desperately trying to equip and train its armed forces. The training schedules that were used early on constantly changed. This was mainly a function of the difference in training school background among the supervisory personnel, and the attempts on the part of the training department to find out what worked best.

Typically, students flew in the morning one day and the afternoon the next, and for a while Sunday was used as a normal training day. Later, Sundays were used only when missed training needed to be made up and the time was not available elsewhere in the schedule.

Ground school instruction consisted of the following subjects, Meteorology, Navigation, Code, Aircraft Recognition, Communications, and Instruments. At first, and for several months after, the school was hampered by lack of equipment, training aids, supplies, and the proper facilities. The building had no light, heat, or furniture. The classrooms used mess tables, and folding chairs borrowed from other units on the post. There was little instructional material, and many of the Technical Manuals were obsolete or not applicable. Much was done by improvisation and the use

The base chapel as it appeared on the campus of Williams College. After the war it was moved to the campus and refurbished.

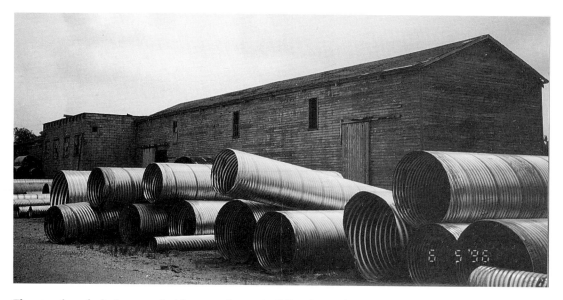

The remains of what was probably a warehouse building located along the railroad track at the former air field.

of "homemade" material. For many months, there were not enough qualified instructors, and to help alleviate the problem, the military commissioned officers directly from civilian schools.

Since, there were few teaching aids available, the ground school made their own. This included a complete set of flying instruments that was made in the Sub-Depot machine shop from scrap material. The school also made a working model of a typical beacon used, at the time, for cross county navigation. It was a little over three feet high, with a rotating light and course lights that flashed a typical coded signal.

Flying training was affected by the many shortages existing at the time of the school's startup. As an example, the maintenance personnel worked twenty-four hours a day, seven days a week keeping the aircraft in the air. Still, they were hampered by a lack of spare parts and equipment, which often resulted in an aircraft being grounded for lack of parts. The corps of flying instructors was a new one, and as expected, their expertise and experience was less than inspiring. As of mid December 1942, the instructors had an experience level of about three and a half months, by March this average had risen to six months. Many of the instructors were not happy to be here. Some had been transferred to the raw, unfinished base at Walnut Ridge from

A classic photo of hundreds of WW II aircraft awaiting their date with the scrap dealer at Walnut Ridge Army Air Field after the war. This photo shows mostly B-17's and B-24's that were flown to the air field. Many retain their combat unit markings. Off in the distance, the north-south runway of the field is clearly visible.

(U.S. AIR FORCE MUSEUM)

existing bases that had more amenities and much better living conditions. They did not look forward to the assignment here doing the same thing they had been doing at their former base, with much better living conditions.

Early classes were obviously affected by the growing pains of the new school, but the students along with their teachers and support personnel made the best of the situation. As the months went by, adjustments were made, and training aids and equipment became available. Also, instructors received additional training and supervision, the courses were standardized, and better facilities became operational. As a result, training reached a high level of efficiency. Just nine months after the school started, it was flying more student hours per month than any other basic flying school in the Eastern Flying Training Command.

The last class of students to graduate from the field was Class 44-H, graduating on June 27, 1944 with a total of 245 student officers, cadets, and aviation students. Although the training program at Walnut Ridge lasted less than two years, it did manage to turn out an impressive number of pilots. During its period of operation, August 1942 to June 1944, the school started 5,310 students of which 4,641 finished training and went to Advanced training. That was a graduation rate of a little more than 87%. The field also posted an impressive number of flying hours. From October 1, 1942 thru June 30, 1944, there were about 414,429 hours flown, which is the equivalent of 51,804, eight hour days; however, the training was not without its cost in human life. The base hospital reported that during the September 1942 thru July 1944 period, thirty nine lives were lost because of aircraft crashes. There may

have been more, perhaps some that were not recorded at the Walnut Ridge base hospital.

Toward the end of the training program in April 1944, Colonel Guillett, who had been the base commander since its opening, departed for a new assignment at Kessler Field, Mississippi. He was replaced by Lt. Col. Gerald Kelley who would be here just a short time until late July. It was during this period that the field slowly began to shut down. It appeared that the rumors, circulating since January, that the base would be transferred to the Navy, would be proven true. During the latter part of May and thru late June, the personnel strength of the base was reduced by about 40%. The number of aircraft also declined; in early June, there were 210 aircraft assigned to the field, and by the end of the month there were just 58. In July, Major David Tudor assumed command of the field. Finally on September 1, 1944 the air base was closed and transferred to the Navy Department. For a while the Marines used the base to train Corsair pilots.

At this point, the Reconstruction Finance Corporation (RFC) entered the history of Walnut Ridge Army Air Field. The war was over, and there were huge quantities of surplus military aircraft that had to be either stored, sold, or scrapped. Most aircraft would eventually be scrapped because there was not much civilian demand for obsolete four engine bombers or high performance fighter aircraft. Those that were still of military value existed in quantities far in excess of the needs of the military in peacetime. So Walnut Ridge was one of the former airfields choosen as a temporary aircraft storage site for the Reconstruction Finance Corporation. The RFC was an agency of the government that was involved in the scrapping and disposal of surplus military aircraft. At the time, late 1945, there were five other large RFC storage fields. They were located at Altus and Clinton Oklahoma; Kingman, Arizona; Augusta, Georgia; and Ontario, California. Walnut Ridge was the largest.

The surplus aircraft were flown to Walnut Ridge and then parked in neat rows in the fields near the runways, and any other place where there was room. The planes were left in the open, not tied down, and as a result, the occasional storms

A monument located across the road from the field's administration building, honors the memory of Lt. Robert Swindle. Lt. Swindle was from Walnut Ridge and a bombardier with the 303rd bomb squadron of the 8th Air Force. He was killed in action when his B-17 was shot down during a bombing mission in 1943.

would sometimes cause significant damage to the aircraft. By now, no one cared. This was a far cry from just a few month ago when a career could be ruined if a plane were damaged through an act of carelessness. But the war was over, and at this field alone, sat thousands of aircraft awaiting their fate. It's difficult to say how many were here, but at one time during the scrapping process, the local paper reported that there were 4312 aircraft sitting at the former air base. Not all the planes would be scrapped; some were sold to fledgling airlines, while tons of parts and engines were sold to foreign governments. Some of the aircraft that were at the field during this period included B-17's, B-24's, B-25's, B-26's, B-32's, C-47's, C-54's, P-40's, P-47's, P-51's, BT-13's and probably some BT-15's. Many of the aircraft were combat veterans that had aluminum patches to cover the holes made by enemy bullets and damage caused by flak. Their names included *Fabulous Fannie, Problem Child, Mission Completed, Manhattan Maiden,* and the *Dragon Lady.*

Some of the people who remember the storage and later the scrapping of the thousands of aircraft at Walnut Ridge are Harlon and Glenda Jones, and Bill Flippo. Glenda recalls walking through the aircraft and seeing some of the personal items left by the crews, items such as photos, pocket combs and chewing gum wrappers.

During August 1946, the government awarded a contract to the Texas Railway Equipment Company for the scrapping of 4890 aircraft at the former Walnut Ridge Army Air Field. The smelting operation was set up near or at the former sub-depot hangar which some referred to as the "76 Building." Before cutting the aircraft up, they were stripped of useful equipment and the technical manuals and other papers were taken from the planes and burned. Security was set up to help insure that tools, radios, clocks, and other items of value were not stolen from the planes by the workers and others who were around the field. There also was a car check station. On occasion, people would throw parts that had been taken from the planes, out of their cars when the auto approached the check point. Before the planes were scrapped, the valuable high octane fuel in their tanks was drained and later sold. One newspaper report indicated that about a million and half gallons of gas were drained from the tanks.

In January 1950, Walnut Ridge Army Air Field was turned over to the City of Walnut Ridge and later named Swindle Field. The name honors the memory of Lt. Robert J. Swindle of Walnut Ridge who was a bombardier with the 303rd Bomb Squadron of the 8th Air Force. Lt. Swindle was killed in action when his B-17 was shot down during a bombing raid during 1943. There is an attractive monument to his memory located across the road from the field's administration building. Today the field is a regional airport and is maintained in excellent condition. Some buildings remaining as of 1996 include the sub-depot hangar, another hangar that houses a manufacturing firm, a former mess hall, and the chapel. The chapel has been moved from its original location to the campus of the Williams Baptist College which occupies part of the original air field property. Also remaining is the former base commander's home which appears much as it did in 1945.

9

The Rattlesnake Bomber Base

B-29 TRAINING—PYOTE ARMY AIR FIELD

Situated in the middle of the desolate, open country of West Texas was a sprawling WW II Air Force training facility named Pyote Army Air Field. Surrounded by mesquite, sand, and rattlesnakes, the field had hundreds of buildings, three runways (two about 8400 feet long), gunnery and bombing ranges; all would be used to train thousands of crewmen for the B-17 and the B-29. Pyote Army Air Field was a small city that during April 1945, had a total of 6227 officers and enlisted men permanently assigned or temporally attached to the base. In addition, there were hundreds of civilians that came from all over to work on this 2700 acre base. Like everything else in Texas, Pyote Army Air Field was big.

Today it's gone. Virtually nothing remains that would tell the casual observer that this was once a major training center responsible for turning out highly trained flying crews. The runways and aircraft parking ramp are still here as are the walls of a multi story hangar. There were once six huge hangars fronting the concrete ramp that today has sand blowing across it and weeds growing through the cracks. Everywhere brush is slowly obscuring the many crumbling building foundations found scattered about the former base. One has to be careful walking among the

ruins because the rattlesnakes have retaken their former home and do not like visitors. The original entrance has been refurbished, and today stands as a memorial to the men and women who worked and trained here, many of whom gave their lives while learning to effectively use the B-17 and B-29. Still others who trained here went to war and paid the ultimate price.

The first impression most everyone had of Pyote Army Air Base was its isolation and desert like surroundings. The nearest town, Pyote, had a population of about 200 and just a few stores. Down the road was Monahans, with a population of about 1000. The nearest large town was Pecos, about 25 miles east of the field. One common saying was " if someone went AWOL, the MPs could watch them for several days before they had to go out and pick them up." One of the early arrivals was Jim Carr, a member of the famed 19th Bombardment Group who arrived at Pyote by train in January 1943. He remembers being "dismayed to see the state of construction being carried out there in the desert. There was a sand storm in progress and you could hardly see your hand in front of your face. Tumble weeds were blowing all over the place. And the little town of Pyote (not a town at all but just a whistle stop) was situated about a half

A look at the ramp and some of the cantonment area of Pyote Army Air Field. This photo was probably taken during late 1944 or early 1945. Note the mix of B17's and B-29's. Only the walls of the hangar located at the bottom of the picture survive today. This was the 3rd Echelon Maintenance hangar. The photo gives an excellent view of the celestial navigation towers. There are four and can be seen between and to the rear of the first two hangars. (JIMMY MARKS)

a mile down the road from the main gate. It consisted of a filling station, a greasy spoon restaurant with a small bar, and that was it!" At the time, the base was still in the early stages of construction so there were no hangars, few barracks, and the base theater had wooden benches instead of individual seats. Later, during another sand storm Jim was walking to the post office and decided to wear his gas mask to help protect against the sand carried on the howling wind; however, before going very far, he was stopped by an officer and told not to wear the gas mask because the sand might ruin the canister. Never mind Jim's eyes, nose, and the nasty effect the sand had on his lungs. A chaplain assigned to the 381st Bombardment Group walked from the train station to Pyote, about two miles, and had to empty the sand from his shoes when he entered the base. He then walked through the sand to his barracks, where he wrote his name

in the sand that covered his bed. This was ideal rattlesnake country. A sign posted at the entrance to the base during its construction warned "Beware Rattlesnakes—Wear boots or high top shoes or leggins, Wear protective gloves, Watch where you step, Watch where you reach." For emphasis, the sign had two rattlesnakes drawn on it. It wasn't long before the base got its unofficial name, "Rattlesnake Bomber Base."

Base construction started on September 5, 1942, and within a month, excavation was in progress on the base's runways. Construction was well underway, when the base's first commander, then Major Clarence L. Hewitt, arrived on the site and set up a temporary office in the corner of a just finished warehouse. This was early October and the field was starting to slowly fill with the support personnel necessary to carry out its training mission. The first heavy aircraft, a C-47, landed in October. Since there were as

yet no housing facilities on the base, the early arriving personnel lived in the nearby towns and commuted to and from the base in the back of army trucks. Major Hewitt arrived on October 9, and the first pilot assigned to Pyote, 1st Lieutenant Lloyd Taylor, came on the 21st.

Toward the end of October, the first medical personnel were assigned to the field. Their experiences were probably typical of the first units assigned to the base during the early construction phase. There were no paved roads, no medical vehicles, and the first office was set up in a medical supply warehouse. Here, sick call was held with the personal equipment of the few medical officers assigned to the base, supplemented with some items bought from the local pharmacies. Since the medical warehouse was the only nearly completed warehouse in early November, it was soon filled with base equipment, not necessarily medical supplies. This included, 500 lb. bombs, 50 caliber machine gun ammunition, beds, chairs, rifles, field telephones, and chemical warfare decontamination equipment. By mid November, the hospital was still under construction, missing floors, windows, and doors. At about this time, more than 30 tons of medical supplies arrived that had to be unloaded from the freight cars within 48 hours. So the medical officers, veterinarian, supply officer, and two enlisted men unloaded it using a small truck and a hand cart borrowed from the local railroad station. There were no toilet facilities available for the stenographers, so twice a day, the civilian stenographers were transported by ambulance to a proper facility about a mile from the hospital, near the main gate, and then returned to their offices. The construction of

The ramp and runways of the former air base as they were in 1997. The foundations for the five hangars are clearly visible. The small white space standing by itself on the left edge of the photo behind the hangars may be the remains of the Officer's Club swimming pool. (ISABELLE BLANCHARD, PECOS AIR CENTER)

On final approach to the ramp at Pyote Army Air Field. What remains of the hangars and former cantonment area is to the left of the ramp. (ISABELLE BLANCHARD, PECOS AIR CENTER)

the hospital was nearing completion by the end of December. This would be none too soon, because the first tenants, the 19th Bombardment Group would arrive by the first of 1943. The base was officially opened on Tuesday, January 5, 1942 with ceremonies that included a parade of the base personnel.

The mission of Pyote Army Air Field was to train bomber crews, and much of this early training was done by men of the famed 19th Bombardment Group. This group, which started training of B-17 combat crews in January 1943, had been in combat since the first days of the war. Highly decorated with (at the time) six Distinguished Unit

Citations, the group had seen its first combat when the Japanese attacked Clark Field on December 7, 1941 (December 8 in the Philippines). With the planes not damaged in the attack and the ones able to be repaired, the group flew combat and critically important reconnaissance missions against Japanese shipping and invasion forces. After about two weeks and heavy losses, the group's ground personnel joined the infantry to help fight the invaders. Most of these men were either killed or captured. By late December, the air echelon moved to Australia, and later Java where they continued to fight. The group evacuated Gen. MacArthur, his family, and important members of his staff from the Philippines to Australia, participated in the Battle of the Coral Sea and many other engagements.

As mentioned, when the 19th Bombardment Group ar-

What's left of the 3rd Echelon Maintenance hangar. The small block like structure to the right is the vault where the then secret Norden bombsights were stored. In the distance behind the hangar is the original water tower.

(ISABELLE BLANCHARD, PECOS AIR CENTER)

rived at Pyote Army Air Field, parts of it were still under construction. Regardless, training began and everyone did the best they could even though there was a lack of equipment and proper facilities. Jim Carr, who had seen combat with the 19th Bomb Group as an engineer gunner, recalls that most of the twelve B-17's used to transport the flying crews back from the South Pacific went to Pyote and were used for training. Conditions on the new base were primitive; there were no hangars and not enough barracks, so for a while, he lived in a tent. By now he was a ground crew chief, responsible for the maintenance of a B-17. As Jim explains, "working conditions on the line without hangars were appalling. I remember it took me three days to change an engine in my B-17, a task which should have been done in less than one day. And the rattlesnakes were so bad that we had to be careful working at night because the snakes would crawl in on the ramp to take advantage of the heat retained from the day's sun. You had to look before climbing down off the engine stand or you might step right on a big diamond back rattler." After a while, Jim's crew was working twelve hours a day, seven days a week, with no days off. His shift was from 7 A.M. to 7 P.M. Once he was awakened from a sound sleep and told to hurry and dress because he was late for his shift. After throwing on his coveralls and rushing down the street toward the hangar, he noticed some men playing soft ball and other men sitting on the steps reading a newspaper. This was rather unusual activity for 7 A.M. It soon became apparent that it was seven in the evening, not the morning. Working a twelve-hour shift was not only fatiguing, but confusing as well.

The responsibility of the person-

nel assigned to the base, along with the hundreds of civilian workers, was to provide the food, clothing, housing, maintenance, and supplies necessary for the groups being trained. This included the planes, medical care, weather information, guns, bombs, and special needs such as emergency aid, religious guidance, and security. Along with the instructors of the 19th Bombardment Group, the base had other instructors assigned to help with the training.

Since Pyote AAF was a crew training base, every crew member received training. This included pilot, navigator, gunner, radio operator, and bombardier training. The crew members who arrived at Pyote for training had received preliminary training in their speciality, and here they would become a member of a crew and their skills polished with further training and practice. Assisting the instructors of the 19th Bomb Group were "Model-Crew" members. These men were recent graduates of the three phase training program, sent to Pyote as a "Model Crew." There they would instruct their trainee counterpart by flying training missions with him. For example, a "Model Crew" pilot would fly with a trainee pilot, a "Model Crew" gunner with a trainee gunner, etc.

One of the problems associated with the use of returned combat veterans for training at a

The former hangar as seen from the ramp. The building behind it is the boiler room.

107

military courtesy and customs would be shown three times a day. The base commander, Col. Hewitt said the restriction would be lifted when "the proper corrections have been made."

If this plan didn't work, then individual violators would be summoned to the base commander for personal reprimand, and not released until the unit commander picked up the offender. This procedure was outlined in Base Memorandum No.241 and called "Plan No. 2." Apparently the first phase (restrictions) didn't work, so "Plan No.2" was put into effect. This seemed to work because " infractions reached a new low." The base newspaper reported this fact in its issue of July 28, 1943, when 81 violators were required to "visit" the base commander's office.

By August 1943, the field had been open about seven months and training was in full swing, on a twenty-four hour a day basis. A few months earlier in June, Bill Switzer arrived around midnight, during a rain storm, and was told there were no orders for him to be there. It was soon straightened out, and as Bill recalls

stateside base was their lackadaisical attitude toward military courtesy, proper wearing of the uniform, and military discipline. These men had seen combat, put their lives on the line on a daily basis, and were not impressed with the spit and polish routine of a base far removed from combat. They knew their job, most did it very well, but were not inclined to polish their brass, shine shoes, or salute superior officers, especially young officers, who as yet, had not seen combat. This attitude could set a bad example for the trainees, so steps were taken to help insure a more military appearance by all the personnel assigned to Pyote. One step that was reported in the base newspaper *The Rattler* during mid 1943, said "Beginning today at 1200—and until 'further notice'—all military personnel, living on or off the base is restricted to the limits of the Rattlesnake bomber Base. Reason: "This action has become necessary in order to correct certain deficiencies of training, such as military courtesy and discipline, proper wearing of the uniform, etc." The article went on to say that commanders will use the opportunity to conduct schools and drill on military courtesy, and a film on

Remains of building foundations with the original water tower in the distance. (ISABELLE BLANCHARD, PECOS AIR CENTER)

he "spent the following three years in the wrong end of Texas." He was assigned to a Link trainer building, which was a lucky break for him. These buildings were air conditioned and kept at a constant 78 degrees because the equipment required it. Outside during the summer, the temperature would range from 110 degrees in the barracks to 140 degrees on the ramp. On occasion Bill worked the night shift, 1 A.M. to 9 A.M., and spent some time as an operator in the Celestial Navigation Towers (at this time, Pyote had four). These were quite sophisticated training devices for their day, housed in octagon-shaped towers located near the ramp, just behind the hangars. The short name for them was Navitrainer. They were designed to help a navigator improve his skills by flying simulated cross country flights without leaving the ground. The trainee entered through a door at the bottom of the silo type structure that opened to stairs. The stairs lead up about twenty or more feet to a cockpit like device that held three people, and sat under a starlit dome. Under the cockpit was a large glass plate on which was shown the landscape of the land over which the navigator was "flying." The navigator could plot his course by looking overhead at the stars projected on the ceiling of the silo, or by looking at the "countryside" which was shown on the screen under the "cockpit." Bill Switzer recalls that the trainers were also used for pilot and bombardier training. He was 19 years old at the time, and one of the reasons he was able to instruct the B-17 pilots and bombardiers was that they were about his age. The B-17 pilots were, at the most, 1st Lieutenants. Later on, with B-29, training the command pilots were Majors or Lt. Colonels, some of whom were West Point graduates.

More foundation remains.

In October 1943, during a Second Air Force reorganization, Colonel Louie Turner, formerly commanding officer of the 19th Bombardment Group, became commander (Station Commandant) of Pyote. The former base commander, Colonel Hewitt, went to Walker Army Air Base, Kansas as its new commanding officer. Pyote would continue to train bomber crews; however, with the change, men would now report to a base from their training school, be formed into a crew, and then train together as a team to further refine their skills. After that, the crews would then be processed at another base for combat deploy-

The Officer's Club swimming pool is still here, but the 3rd Echelon Maintenance hangar in the distance was torn down and today only the side walls remain. The picture was taken around 1986. (JIMMY MARKS)

A 1986 photo of the remains of the fountain that was in front of the Officer's club. (JIMMY MARKS)

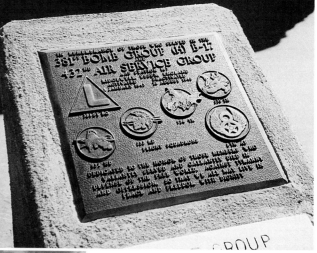

Above: Two plaques which stand at the gate to honor the memory of the men and women who served here.

This is the main gate as it was circa 1945. Part of the gate was built by German prisoners of war. The sign on one side of the field stone wall reads "Rattlesnake" the other side says "Bomber Base." (JIMMY MARKS)

ment. Under the old system, in some cases, training was spread out over three different stations. Pyote Army Air Base would now be known officially as a Bombardment Crew Training School. The training program was now broken down into three parts, Military Training, Ground Training, and Flying Training. The consolidation and reorganization was phased in on a gradual basis, becoming effective on a broad scale during early November 1943. The purpose of the change was to make the training of heavy bombardment crews more efficient and reduce the number of people necessary to run an air base.

The gate after being restored and as it was in 1997.

The base's first Open House was held in early October about ten months after it opened, and was attended by more than 4000 people from the surrounding towns. Aircraft were on display, including a B-17 that had a ramp built around it so the visitors, many of whom had never seen the bomber, could get an up close view. Open Houses were common at the training bases, generally happening once a year. They gave the public an opportunity to see what their War Bonds were paying for, and also helped develop better understanding between the military and the civilians of the nearby towns. Pyote's first Open House had a unique way to encourage the purchase of War Bonds by offering a free Jeep ride to those who bought bonds during the show. About $1,000 worth of bonds were sold.

By February 1944, about a year after the base opened, the training of bomber crews at Pyote was being handled by the 19th Combat Crew Training School. By then, the reorganization directed by the 2nd Air Force the previous October, had been implemented at the base. The training program for the men assigned to Pyote followed the same procedure. All crew members received training in their speciality, (i.e. pilots, bom-

bardiers, navigators, engineers, radio operators and gunners,) during a three-phase program. Each phase was about a month long, and had minimum requirements that were supposed to be met before the crew could be sent into combat. During the first phase, a transition period, the pilot met his crew and they begin working together to learn about the B-17. (Crew members were normally assigned simply by checking names off alphabetical rosters) Individual crew members received instruction in their specialities, which included ground instruction as well as aerial training. During the second phase, teamwork was emphasized with bombing, gunnery, and instrument flight missions flown by full crews. The last phase included high altitude formation flying, long range navigation, and simulated combat missions.

All training was subdivided under three Directors; Flying, Ground, and Military, each of

A B-29 in the process of being scrapped December 1945. This particular ship had its gear fail on landing. (P.J. MCLAUGHLIN)

After WW II, Pyote Army Air Field served as a temporary storage center for hundreds of aircraft including B-29's. Some of the B-29's arrived brand new from the production line, while others were combat veterans from Guam, Tinian, and Saipan. While some of the B-29's returned to the air via SAC, and perhaps elsewhere, many others were scrapped. This view shows them having been cocooned and now waiting to be scrapped. (JIMMY MARKS)

whom reported to the Director of Training. There was also a Standardization Board which worked to insure the quality of the instructors and maintain standardized and efficient instruction. At this time, the majority of instructors at Pyote were combat veterans. While this overview of the training program sounds simplistic; it was actually quite complex. For example, gunnery instruction required ten ranges where more than 300 men per day fired a variety of weapons including the .50 caliber machine gun. Aerial gunnery instruction needed aircraft to tow targets (in early 1943, they used AT-23's—converted Martin B-26's). Fighter aircraft were used to make mock attacks on the B-17's so the gunners could learn to track fighters. The gunnery school had 48 instructors, operated twelve hours daily, and was one of eight in the Ground Training Program. By early February 1944, after the base had been in operation a little over a year, 84,871 hours had been flown at the base. That's equivalent to about 10,609 eight-hour days.

There were, however, problems with the training. There were not enough planes for the instruc-

tor pilots to practice with, navigators were not receiving enough practice, and flights were not long enough to allow bombardiers sufficient time to improve their skills. At the end of March, the field was redesignated, the 236th AAF Base Unit (Combat Crew Training School) (Heavy). This replaced the 19th Combat Crew Training School and was primarily an administrative change. At the end of April, Pyote had 3,556 people assigned and according to an aircraft status report for June 1944, there were, on average, about 56 airplanes on the base. During June, about 36 planes were available for flying, and these flew almost nine hours per day, handling the training for 142 crews. It was at this time that a significant change in the training mission of the base was about to take place. On July 8, two B-29's landed at Pyote, and less than two months later (August 15) the base became a "very heavy" training station and part of the 16th Bomb Wing. Slowly, B-17 instruction would be phased out and replaced by B-29 training.

This was a major change for the base because the B-29 was a totally different aircraft. It was a highly complex, state of the art bomber, that incorporated many new and innovative features which, at the time, were causing serious operational and safety problems. Engine fires were common. Hurried into production, without the normal testing, the plane had major teething problems, some of which would plague the bomber throughout the war. Yet it offered so much more in the way of improved performance, crew comfort (it was pressurized), range, and bomb carrying capability, that the risk of rushing it into combat seemed justified. The aircraft dwarfed the B-17. The B-29 weighed approximately 70,000 lbs. empty, compared to the B-17G's, 36,000 lbs. Its

113

Some of the other types of aircraft stored at Pyote. This photo taken in March 1946 shows a liaison aircraft damaged when its tie down ropes broke during a windstorm. (P.J. MCLAUGHLIN)

wingspan was about 141 feet, compared to the B-17's 103 feet. While the B-17G was powered by four 1200 HP engines, the B-29 had four 2200 HP engines. The only major thing common to the two was that they were both designed and built by Boeing. Pyote Army Air Field prepared to switch from training on a long existing, proven aircraft to a radical new one with serious operational problems, and few personnel experienced or trained in their maintenance and operation. The challenge would be interesting.

The school was now under the command of Colonel Bernard Castor, and this would be his first experience with a four-engine training field. July was made interesting for Col. Castor, because the mission to train B-29 crews was canceled (at the time it was called the B-I project) and transferred to Biggs Field in El Paso, Texas. This meant that all the information, parts, and other items needed for the B-29 program either on order, or already in place at Pyote, had to be sent back and the orders canceled. Then, later in the month, the project was reassigned to the base and the process started over again. As a

result, the Supply and Equipment sections were kept busy shipping B-17 equipment and planes to Biggs Field, while receiving B-29 material from all over the United States.

John Copeland remembers the B-29's, especially the one that was involved in a spectacular accident. After dinner one evening, John and his friends were in their barracks located near the flight line, when they heard a B-29 fly over very low. After going out to look, they noticed the plane's number 3 engine on fire. The pilot decided to land the plane, and extended the gear; however, the tires on one side had been burned. As a result, when landing, the B-29 turned 90 degrees and, out of control, went crashing through several smaller aircraft parked in the transient part of the flight line. Continuing on its journey, the out of control plane now headed for the dispatcher's office. Here it stopped when the nose gear collapsed. The only casualties were the tail gunner who had a broken ankle as a result of his jumping from the rear door, and the dispatch crew that was still running the next morning. Jim and his friends got a chance to play fireman that night,

There were hundreds of RP-63's stored at Pyote. This picture taken in July 1946 gives a nice direct view of one sitting in front of the control tower. (P.J. MCLAUGHLIN)

putting out the many small fires started by the plane. Fortunately, there was not that much fuel because the plane was returning from a mission and had dumped some prior to the landing.

August was a transition month for the base, when training was being phased out on the B-17 and preparations were in the final stage for the training of B-29 crews. By September 1, twenty crews were being trained on the new bomber; however, training was hampered by a severe shortage of experienced personnel, both to maintain the aircraft and instruct the trainees. Adding to the problem was a lack of B-29's. One class, PY 1-24, was forced to stop training and the trainees were sent on leave because there were not enough aircraft. To help fix some of the problems, experts were sent to Pyote to help build training aids, and teach the instructors how to use them. Other personnel were given training at various installations. By

mid-September, the first B-29 engineering mockups, used for instruction in the B-29 systems, arrived. Reflecting the shortage of aircraft and the difficulty keeping them flying, the field had, on average, about ten B-29's during September, of which less than four were available for flight. The field still had about sixteen B-17's. The B-17's would remain on the field for some time and be used in the B-29 training program. This was not an ideal solution for training B-29 crews; however, there was little choice because sufficient B-29's, parts, and experienced personnel were not available. Because of the shortage of trained personnel and training equipment, three classes were held over during November for an additional month's training. One class, already processed, packed, and ready to board the troop train for Kearney Army Air Field, was recalled for training. Later on, the classes were set back again with the addition of

115

additional members. Two training facilities that were not available were a radar bombing target and an air to ground gunnery range large enough to accommodate the B-29. The original range, built for the B-17, was four miles wide; the B-29 required one that was five miles wide. This would allow the plane to fly over the middle of the range so all gunners could fire simultaneously. In December, most of the planes were grounded for modifications and engine changes.

Jim Carr, working in maintenance at the time, remembers the long hours necessary to keep the planes in service. The maintenance crews were working twenty four hours around the clock, and would start a new inspection when they started their shift. They would remain on the shift until the inspection was finished, no matter how long it took. An amusing incident happened around two or three A.M. It involved a B-29 that had finished inspection and needed to be delivered to the other end of the ramp about a mile away. So, hooking up the short tow bar of his tractor to the front gear strut of the plane, Jim began towing the plane. It was dark, the wind was blowing in what seemed like a gale, helping to push the B-29 along. Jim was in a hurry to deliver the plane and get off work, so he drove the tractor as fast as it would go. Another man was in the cockpit on the brakes of the plane when Jim heard what he thought was the tow bar fall off the plane. His tractor was only about two or three feet from this huge plane, which he now thought was out of control and doing its best to run over and crush him. He yelled for his friend in the cockpit to hit the brakes. Even though Jim had the tractor's gas pedal to the floor, it looked like the plane was getting closer and closer. At last, the man in the cockpit heard Jim and slammed on the brakes. Everything came to a sudden stop, except Jim who went sailing over the top of the tractor onto the concrete ramp. Later on, he realized the noise he heard was not the tow bar, but a spare one carried on the tractor.

A particularly sad accident happened on January 3, 1945, when Lieutenant John Jamison was killed instantly when he was hit by a spinning propeller during an inspection. Lt. Jamison had served in the European Theater as a B-17 pilot and had survived 25 combat missions. He was the recipient of the Distinguished Flying Cross, and the Air Medal with three Oak Leaf Clusters.

The first class to finish their B-29 combat crew training (PY-1-24) left Pyote Army Air Field on January 24, 1945. The class had 35 crews and went to two staging bases, some to Kearney Army Air Field in Nebraska, and the others to Herington Army Air Field in Kansas. This was considered the "guinea pig" class. Originally scheduled to take three months, it took five. This, of course, was a reflection of the problems associated with the start up of the B-29 training program at Pyote caused by the need to get the B-29 into combat as soon as possible. Some of the problems included a lack of equipment, inadequate/non-existent facilities, not enough trained instructors or mechanics, and other personnel necessary to run an air base. As late as February 1945, training was still hampered by a lack of material and equipment. For example, air to ground gunnery practice was halted because of the lack of sixty dummy aircraft, ordered in December, for the air to ground gunnery range. Most of the navigation officers received little if any training in the Celestial Navigation trainer because there were no Air Almanacs available. It is unknown if the training was made up later at Pyote, or was accomplished by the crew at a different station. A report in March by the Standardization Board summed up the training situation: " . . . several crew members were required to accomplish certain things in the air in which they never had ground instruction, —Extreme pressure is being exerted from higher headquarters to accomplish maximum training in a minimum amount of time. This causes the Training Squadron to accept a poor performance of a mission as satisfactory . . ."

It should be emphasized that probably much of the missed training was not critical, and may have been made up later. At this point in the war, some of the training may not even have been necessary. Only those who were there can speak to that point. Also, after the crews left Pyote, additional training took place, some at the staging bases. No doubt the B-29 training, not only at Pyote, but at all the B-29 bases, could have been more thorough; however, the B-29's and their crews were needed for the air war over Japan, and to delay them would have prolonged the war. At the end of April, one month before the war was finished in Europe, there were 6227 officers and enlisted men assigned or taking training at the base. During July 1945, the base set a flying time record of 7,396 hours. This was the greatest number of hours ever flown in any one month by a B-29 crew training station and amounted, to about 925 eight-hour days.

With the end of the war against Japan, training became less intense, and over time was gradually phased out. During August, the maintenance personnel switched from working 24 hours a day to two shifts per day. Also around this time, the base personnel were put on a five and a half day work week instead of the former one day off every ten days. By now, many were concerned about their prospects for occupation duty in Japan, or how soon they could be separated from the service.

During November 1945, Pyote Army Air Field was transferred from the Second Air Force to the San Antonio Air Technical Service Command. The 236th AAF Base Unit was discontinued. The new mission of the base was to store aircraft which included B-29's, P-63's, L-4's and L-5's. Later on there were B-25's, B-17's and AT-7's. Military personnel on the field in mid-November totaled 2897, and by December this had dropped to 1181. With the decrease in activity and the significant reduction of people working on the field, it was rapidly taking on the air of a ghost town. The aircraft continued to arrive at Pyote, and by the end of December, there were 989 aircraft in storage at the base, 742 of which were B-29's. The B-29's had come from Guam, Tinian, Saipan, and new production from the Boeing plants at Renton Washington, and Wichita, Kansas. Aircraft continued to arrive after December and the number on the field fluctuated. They were parked ev-

erywhere, on taxiways, the ramp, in the fields surrounding the runways, and even on a runway. For a while the "Enola Gay" was stored here as was "Alexander the Swoose," the only B-17 that served with the 19th Bomb Group and survived to return to the United States. Both are now in the Smithsonian Institution. The number of aircraft stored here reached a peak in late 1948 when there were just over 2000.

Aircraft storage and the cocooning of some of these planes was the last major activity at Pyote Army Air Field. Storage included not only preserving planes for future use but also transferring some of the stored planes to other Air Force units for their use. For example, many of the B-29's stored at Pyote would again see service in the Korean war and would be flown by the men of the 19th Bomb Group. This is the same group that was the first to serve at Pyote Army Air Base. Eventually, the aircraft remaining at Pyote were scrapped when it was apparent there would be no further use for them.

So, with the aircraft gone, there was little use for the Rattlesnake Bomber Base. There was a radar station here for a while starting in 1958, but the entire facility was too large and outmoded to maintain. In 1966, it was turned over to the General Services Administration for disposal.

Today in the town of Pyote, about 15 miles west of Monahans, there is a museum honoring the memory of the men and women who served here. Founded in large part through the efforts of Jim Marks, it is devoted to the history of the field, and contains photographs, uniforms, and other World War II memorabilia. Jim Marks has been interested in the former air base since he was a child and first saw the hundreds of aircraft stored at the field. A retired Colonel, Jim served in Korea where he received the Silver Star for gallantry in action, the Bronze Star for valor, two Purple Hearts, as well as 5 battle stars and the U.S. and Korean Presidential Unit Citations. For those interested in the field, the museum is well worth the visit. Open on Saturday and Sunday; appointments to visit at other times can probably be made by phoning ahead.

The Battle of Kansas

Pratt Army Air Field

Pratt Army Air Field was located about three miles north of the city of Pratt, Kansas on approximately 2600 acres of flat Kansas prairie. Here, the 40th Bombardment Group would receive its training and be among the first to take the B-29 to war. But before this could happen much had to be done to get the B-29's and their crews ready for combat.

Pratt AAF was one of the first to receive a B-29, actually a YB-29, one of the earliest models of the new bomber. The plane was flown there by Colonel Lewis Parker in the summer of 1943 to begin forming the 40th Bomb Group. The

airbase at Pratt was one of four fields, all located in Kansas, used to train the newly created 58th Bomb Wing, (Very Heavy). The others were: Walker Army Air Field, Victoria, Kansas; Great Bend Army Air Field, Great Bend, Kansas; and Smoky Hill Army Air Field, Salina, Kansas. Another Kansas field involved with the B-29 was Herington Army Air Field, Herington,

One of the two still existing WW II hangars remaining from Pratt Army Air Field.

Kansas. Here about 60 per cent of all the B-29's and crews that went overseas were processed prior to their leaving the United States.

All this was in the future when construction of Pratt Army Air Field officially began in September 1942. Originally, the field was intended to process crews and equipment for overseas assignment; however, the need for B-29 training bases changed this. Some of the earliest military personnel to arrive at the site of the new airbase were the Army Engineers. They set up their office at the Peoples Bank in town, and later moved to the Pratt Motor Company on South Main. The first building erected on the field's site was the engineer's building, and from there, the construction of the base would be directed. Grading the field started in October 1942, and during the time the field was under construction, the announcement was made that it would be expanded. This was a major expansion that prepared the field for the role it would play in getting the B-29's and their crews ready for combat. Eventually, the new airbase would have three runways, each 8000 feet long, and five hangars. The official dedication took place in May 1943, with approximately 13,000 people attending the ceremony. In just a few months, a small city had been built about four miles north of the city of Pratt, that at the time had a population of approximately seven thousand people. The field's first commanding officer was Lieutenant Colonel John Nelson.

The huge increase in people, both construction workers and newly arriving military personnel, put an extraordinary demand on the limited housing facilities in and around the city of Pratt. As a result, all the unoccupied apartments and spare rooms were soon rented to the new arrivals; the lack of housing became a serious problem. To help meet the need for more space, many of the homeowners converted their basements and other spare rooms into living space.

Mrs. Dorotha Giannangelo remembers the housing problems very well; she said, "if you could divide a room and get two, then you did that. Everything was filled in the town all the time the base was there." At the time, Dorotha was a college student majoring in theater and English at the University of Iowa, and for a time worked as a secretary at the air base. Dorotha recalls; " It was a small town and everyone knew that my mother had a three room studio in the home. It was the peer pressure that caused her to rent one of the rooms because it was felt she didn't need three rooms." That's how Dorotha met her husband; the man who rented the room was a dentist moving into Pratt to practice dentistry.

Opening up spare rooms for rent helped but didn't solve the problem, so the Federal Government tried several initiatives. One of the first was to build a trailer park, and by July 1943, 217 trailers were being moved to the site. Each trailer had a stove, refrigerator, and a couch that converted to a bed. The trailers could sleep two people, and others could be expanded to sleep up to six people. The trailers had electric lights, but no running water or toilet facilities. The toilets and bathing facilities were located in a separate building near where the trailers were parked; however, most of the trailers had been used before and had to be cleaned and repaired before they could be used again. Another housing project, started in July 1943 and later named Victory Heights, had 120 living units for employees of the government. The housing area covered four square blocks, and consisted of about 25 buildings. The homes were rectangular in

An aerial view of the ramp and cantonment area of Pratt Army Air Field, circa 1945.

ing, and long range missions were practiced along with the many other tasks necessary to build an effective fighting group. In April 1944, as a result of a Second Air Force change, the base would handle not only the housekeeping for the groups, but also be responsible for training. It took some time to make the necessary changes, and it was not until August 1944, that the revised training system was put into practice with the 29th Group. The B-29 groups trained at Pratt Army Air Field were the 40th, the 497th, the 29th, the 346th, and finally the 93rd. The base was inactivated in December 1945.

shape with flat roofs, and were made of cement blocks. Some buildings had six apartments, while others had four. The units had showers, gas for cooking and hot water, and were heated by a coal burning stove. Although spartan, they were much more comfortable than the trailers. Most of the buildings, after some refurbishing, were still in use as late as 1965 as low income homes. Later, a rest home was built on the site, and two of the original dwellings were remodeled. The other units were torn down. Today the site is the location of the Hampton-Pennock Park and the Friendship Manor Rest Home. Three of the original buildings remain.

When first opened, the base's mission was to provide housekeeping, administrative services, and general support to the bombardment groups at Pratt for combat group training. The newly formed groups conducted their own training. This was the stage of training where the hundreds of men forming the bombardment group learned to function as a team. Individual training continued as necessary to polish skills, but the emphasis was on teamwork. Formation fly-

The training of the B-29 groups at Pratt and the other Kansas air bases was challenging and filled with problems; the major cause was the B-29 itself. A revolutionary new aircraft, the most sophisticated the world had ever seen, was rushed into production because there was an urgent need to get the plane into combat as quickly as possible. As a result, everything connected with the B-29 and the crews to fly it was done at breakneck speed. Of course, there would be mistakes. For example, the first B-29's off the assembly line were not fit for combat. One of the problems was that the engines tended to overheat and burn at a most discouraging rate. In addition to the many faults in the aircraft was a lack of trained personnel to build, maintain, and fly it. This training was further hampered by the lack of B-29's and the appropriate training aids. Many of the early gunners were trained using specially modified B-24's (when available) to master the B-29's intricate fire control system. Also to help ease the problem, other aircraft types, such as the B-17, were substituted for training purposes.

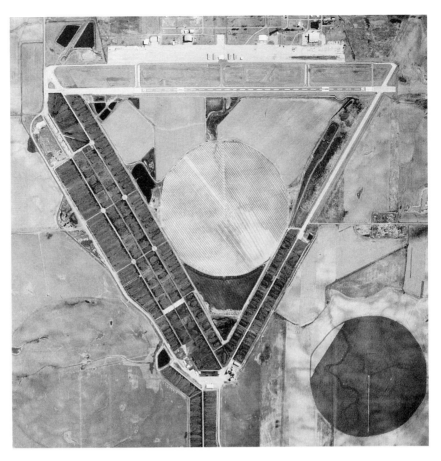

A good indication of the early B-29 training at Pratt Army Air Field is provided by Quenten Hannawald, a civilian employee who worked at the field during this period. He remembers the arrival of the first B-29 (a YB-29) at Pratt in the summer of 1943. At about the same time, the 40th Bomb Group arrived to begin training. The 40th came from the Panama Canal zone where they had operated B-26 Marauders and the B-17. When the YB-29 arrived at Pratt, it was considered top secret and was placed under guard in a hangar. A special pass was required to get near it. At first, the plane was inundated with technicians from Boeing Aircraft, working around the clock correcting electrical and mechanical problems. From time to time, the plane was flown for short periods, only to be followed by seeming endless inspections and modifications. By now, there were a few more B-29's at Pratt, but they seldom flew. One crew member recalls that during the month of January 1944, he flew 79 hours, but only a little over six were in the B-29. Quenten also recalls that at first there were no special tools or stands to work on the B-29's; they had to be made locally in the machine shop, and after being tested, drawings were made for the units using the plane. When the unit went overseas, they would make their own tools using the drawings as a guide. To help speed the design and making of the tools and equipment stands, Quenten and the shop foreman were

Today's entrance to the old air base, which is now Pratt's Municipal Airport.

The former parachute loft as it appears today.

flown to the Boeing factory at Wichita, Kansas to look at the tools Boeing was using.

By late 1943 and early 1944, it became clear that despite heroic efforts to get the B-29 ready for combat there was still a lot that had to be done. Meanwhile, two major modification centers had been set up, one in Georgia, and the other in Alabama, to make changes in the B-29 after they came off the production lines. These changes were the result of deficiencies discovered as the bomber was being tested and entering service. It was faster and more efficient to continue the production of the aircraft with deficiencies and then fly it to a modification center, than to shut down the production line and make the changes there; however, the efforts at the modification centers were still not enough to handle the backlog of newly manufactured aircraft awaiting changes. Most of the problems resulted from the fact that the new, state of the art aircraft was rushed into

production without the luxury of a thorough analysis and testing. Adding to the problem was a lack of material, not enough skilled people to do the work and finally, a general air of confusion about the entire project.

Commitments had been made, however, to get some B-29's into combat by June, and time was running out. So the decision was made to focus resources of men and material at the four Kansas bases, Smoky Hill, Pratt, Great Bend and Walker, to prepare enough B-29s for combat in the China-Burma and India theater. This was the start of the "Battle of Kansas." From all over the country, by train and plane, the necessary men and material were rushed to the four airbases to

On the left of the photo is what was probably the machine shop, and to its right is the sub-depot hangar. On the right of the photo is a front view of the parachute loft.

122

This was probably the former sub-depot hangar that was the largest on the field, as it appears today.

make the many needed changes, some of which included: engine changes, rudder improvements, side sighting dome revisions, fuel gauge modifications, and the installation of flat glass in the cockpit. All of this had to be done in the middle of the flat Kansas prairie near the end of a brutal Kansas winter. Snow was everywhere and the wind came across the prairie with a force that cut to the bone. The bases did not have sufficient hangar space, so considerable work was done outside, night and day, on a twenty-four-hour basis. There were B-29's parked everywhere—in the hangars, on the ramp, even on the taxi strips. To help ease the severity of the cold, hot air gasoline heaters were flown in from all over the country. Still, it was difficult working in the sleet, snow, and the cold winds that caused hands to go numb, making the most simple tasks difficult. Making the situation even more challenging were the long working hours; some men stayed at the job until they could work no longer, went to the barracks to sleep, and then returned back to the line. When a part was needed, the worker just went to the warehouses and took it; no paperwork was required. The only records kept were on the work needing to be completed and the work that was completed. If warmer clothing was required, the men simply went to the quartermaster and asked

for it. On occasion, it was necessary to get parts from cities far away from the airfields, such as Detroit or Birmingham. In those cases, the Air Transport Command flew a plane there and picked it up. The Battle of Kansas started in early March and continued for the next forty four days. Its goal was to have all the required aircraft finished by April 15, 1944, so they could be flown from the airfields to the China, Burma, India Theater, and from there, into combat. Considerable coordination and direction was required among the four bases to insure the effective management of men and material. To do this, part of the base hospital at Smoky Hill was established as the modification headquarters, with General Meyers directing the operation from there.

To help meet the ambitious schedule, Army aircraft flew night and day bringing in the material and manpower necessary to accomplish the job. This included flying in the modified engines that had to be switched with the engines that were currently on the plane. Then the "old' engine was flown to San Antonio or Oklahoma and modified for later use. At Pratt, the 40th Bomb Group personnel helped with and did seven different changes and modifications. These included changing engines, replacing rudders that were not the updated strengthened type, and replacing the main landing gear tires. The men working in the radar section had to install different electronic equipment, but were slowed by the fact that they had

What remains of the bombsight storage vaults today.

The Victory Heights housing complex as it appeared circa 1950.
Today the site is the location of the Hampton-Pennock Park and the Friendship Manor Rest Home.

Some additional buildings remaining on the former airfield today. These were probably warehouses.

never done it before. Other required changes were done by modification personnel working at the field. Even with this unprecedented influx of men and equipment and the twenty-four hour days, the quality and quantity of the work were not satisfactory. The reason was obvious, most of the workers, both military and civilian, did not have the experience and skills necessary to do the job. Many of the workers from the modification centers had only recently been hired and had little or no technical skills.

So, the Army appealed to Boeing for help. This project was not Boeing's responsibility; however, they rushed almost 600 skilled technicians from their production lines at Wichita to the various bases in order to insure the project was completed on time. While all this was going on, the B-29 crews were being processed for the combat zone, attending briefing sessions, getting

their shots, and saying goodbye. Gradually, the necessary changes were finished and aircraft began to leave the bases, first by themselves, and by early April in groups of four or five. By April 15, it was over. The 40th Group had left Pratt and the field went back to its task of training other groups until the end of the war.

On Thursday, October 25, 1945, the headline for the *Pratt Daily Tribune* announced the base would close on December 31. The field would be among nine others inactivated by the Second Air Force. The article mentioned that Col. Rueben Kyle Jr. commanding officer of the field, announced: "It is requested that all business establishments having bills against the government under contracts executed by contracting officers of the Pratt Army Air Field present the same to the contracting officer on or before 1 December 1945 for administration and payment."

One of the independent Living units of Friendship Manor Rest Home that was once part of the Victory Heights complex. Photo taken in 1989.

cluded: barracks, lavatories, administration buildings, warehouses, mess halls, a theater, the Celestial Navigation buildings, the fire station, library, and many others. Any fixtures still remaining in the buildings at the time of the sale were included with the purchase. One hundred and nineteen buildings were sold at this sale. This number did not include buildings that had been sold or were in the process of being sold to priority holders, such as state and local governments and school boards. At that time, there were still about two hundred buildings left on the field that were unsold. Another article in the same paper on August 29 reported that one hundred and sixty nine buildings were sold at a public auction attended by a crowd of about four hundred people. The auction lasted about an hour and a half and was held in the base theater. The base theater, which had 485 seats, and where once soldiers viewed movies, attended meetings, and saw stage shows, was sold for $1,787.

Over the next several months the field was gradually shut down. The 93rd Bomb Group was the last to be trained at the field, and the Group left in December. Two wards of the base hospital were closed, and the PX had a discount sale to reduce its inventory. The USO scheduled its last dance at the Municipal auditorium before its closing on February 28, 1946. The USO had been located in several rooms of the Municipal Building, and opened in March 1943. During its period of operation more than 200,000 soldiers visited the center. On March 6, the last B-29 left the airbase, which by now was down to about 200 men; far from its wartime peak of more than 5000.

Some of the equipment used at the field such as office furniture, plumbing, electrical supplies, typewriters, parachutes, and flying clothing was sold through competitive bids. Over time, many of the buildings and fixtures on the base were declared surplus and sold by the War Assets Administration. The *Pratt Daily Tribune* of July 8, 1947 announced a building sale in which bids were invited for the purchase and removal of the buildings declared surplus. Buildings for sale in-

Today the former air base is the Pratt Municipal Airport and Industrial Park. Several buildings still remain from the World War II era including two of the huge hangars and some concrete vaults where the Norden bomb sights were stored. Two of the three runways have been converted to a cattle feedlot operation, and the open land has returned to farming purposes. The city of Pratt has a wonderful historical society that maintains a fascinating museum about the region's history. The old training base is remembered here, and it's well worth a visit.

11

Advanced Training

Craig Field—Selma, Alabama

If one of the thousands of pilots who took training at Craig Field, were to fly over his old training field today, he would have little trouble recognizing it. Quite a lot of the former air base still remains from World War II. Many of the buildings, some in excellent condition, are still here, as is the lake that separates the former living area from the hangars and flight line. The headquarters building remains, as does the chapel, which is now a branch library. It takes little imagination to visualize the chapel as it was so long ago. Just off to the side of the main entrance road is a T-33 jet trainer mounted on a pylon in a park like setting. The memorial plaque, attached to the pylon, proudly announces—"29th FTW Served Here With Distinction—1940–1977." Several of the barracks where the cadets lived during training are still here, and many of these buildings are in excellent condition. Selma's pride in this historic training center, and its role in WW II is evident in the way the grounds are maintained and the history preserved by the people of Selma.

Craig Field was one of the early training fields built before WW II to accommodate the growing number of pilot trainees. At that time, the Army Air Corps was rapidly expanding and it was clear that additional facilities would be needed for all phases of pilot training. Kelly Field in San Antonio Texas, was handling advanced pilot training,

but would soon be swamped by the additional student pilots. As a result, additional training centers were established, and Craig Field would be the first of the expansion fields to offer advanced single engine training. Craig Field is located about five miles east of Selma, Alabama just off U.S. Highway 80. Originally, the site was open land used primarily for grazing cattle and growing cotton. Situated within the 1986 acre expanse was a pecan grove that still stands today because it was saved from destruction during the building period. The grove was the site of many graduation exercises when the weather permitted the ceremonies to be held out of doors. To obtain the land and make it more favorable for government use, the citizens of Selma purchased it for $140,000 and then leased it back to the government for $1 a year. The population of Selma at the time (1940) was about 20,000 and the building of the field was to be the largest development in the history of Dallas County. Unlike many of the USAAF training fields, this field was built and in operation prior to the outbreak of the war. Craig Field's first class, the 39 cadets of Class 41D, graduated in May 1941, seven months before the WW II. The citizens of Selma wanted the base here and were enthusiastic in their support of it. The naming of the base was important to the city and several names were considered including "Burns Field,"

Some cadets who seem to be happy arriving at Craig Field prior to the beginning of their training.

(USAF VIA OTHA CARNEAL, THE OLD DEPOT)

This picture was probably taken in late 1941 or early 1942 and shows Craig Field's main road looking toward the flight line in the distance. (USAF VIA OTHA CARNEAL, THE OLD DEPOT)

This photo was probably taken in 1941 while training was in progress and the field still under construction. One of the distinguishing characteristics of Craig Field would be the lake between the cantonment area and the flight line. In this picture the lake has not yet formed.

(PAT HUGHEN, SELMA PUBLIC LIBRARY)

to honor Selma's mayor. Another name that was suggested was "Burns-Frasier"; Frasier was the then secretary of the Chamber of Commerce. Also suggested was the name of John T. Morgan, who had served in the United States Senate. The name finally chosen was to honor Bruce Kilpatrick Craig who was killed in a crash of a B-24 in June 1941. He was born in Selma and was a commissioned officer in the Infantry Reserve. At the time of the crash, he was working as a flight test engineer for Consolidated Aircraft Corporation, the manufacturer of the B-24.

The building of Craig Field began in August 1940, and proceeded rapidly so that by December there were about forty structures on the new base. A group of 120 Army personnel commanded by Colonel Vincent Dixon, arrived on August 5 to help with the early construction. Since there were no buildings available, the troops slept in tents and their headquarters was in an old cafe. By December, the runways were under construction and by late 1943, there would be four of them, the longest of which was 5000 feet. Unlike many of the training fields rushed into completion during this period, some of the buildings were of permanent construction. These buildings were not the normal wood frame type covered with tar paper, but were made of a concrete block type material and featured a screened porch that ran across the length of the building. These were rather luxurious accommodations for the time. To make the grounds more attractive and the new field a bit more pleasing to the ca-

dets, many of the mature trees were saved during the construction process. Even though construction had just begun and the field was not ready for training, it was activated as Selma Army Air Base on August 4, 1940. Its mission was the training of aviation cadets in the advanced phase of flying training. This was the last step prior to the cadets receiving their wings as rated pilots. Supposedly, the first plane to land on the field was a Douglas O-38 (an observation plane) flown by a Lt. Bowling who landed in October. The training, which began in early 1941 while the airfield was still under construction, graduated more than 9000 pilots from the advanced flying training program by the end of the war.

Earl Siddens was one of the early arrivals at Craig Field. He remembers checking in at night in March 1941, and spending that first night in the guard house because there were no other accommodations available. He was one of the lucky ones because his barracks was of the semi-permanent type, not a tent or wood frame building that housed some of the other soldiers. At that time, the field was still under construction. One interesting side note is that the barracks Earl lived in is still on the field today. Earl was here until January 1942, and served as a control tower operator. He enjoyed his job and met his wife in Selma. He can still recall the time he tried to warn a cadet that the cadet was about to land

This late 1996 picture shows the flight line separated from the cantonment area by the lake. Many of the aircraft sitting on the ramp were surplus Army Beachcraft UC-21's and C-12's.

Wright Field in Dayton, Ohio, and were a mixture of civilians and military personnel.

Reuben recalls that the runways were not finished and the parking ramp was just half paved. The lake which today is a prominent part of the field was not there; then, it was just a stream about seven feet wide that separated the flight line from the living area. During construction, the stream was dug out and later a dam built which caused the lake to form.

The pilot training in 1941 was on a peace time basis and included a seventy-hour flying course. Included in the flying training were cross country flights, instrument and night flying, and ground and aerial gunnery at Eglin Field, Florida. The ground training was thorough, and covered

his T-6 with the landing gear up. In spite of his attempts to call the pilot over the radio, the airplane landed wheels up and slid to a stop on its belly. Later, Earl was told that the cadet was confused, and could not hear the radio because the landing gear horn was making too much noise!

The training that began in the early spring of 1941 used two temporary runways because the permanent runways were not finished; the first runway would not be done until October. By early May there were about 53 AT-6's assigned to the base along with some other aircraft. During this period, conditions were primitive, meaning that the aircraft maintenance work was done outside. By late April, parts of the parking apron had been completed and some work was being done in the main hangar. Another early arrival at the field was Reuben Bishop who came here as a civilian to work in the sheet metal shop. He came here in June 1941, after completing two years of pre-med school. Reuben remembers his first job was "pushing a broom" and going to school at night (in the sheet metal shop) to learn the sheet metal trade. At that time most of the aircraft maintenance workers (sheet metal workers, mechanics, parachute riggers, etc.) were from

Another aerial that shows the present day runway system and most of the former cantonment area at the top of the picture.

130

A bird's eye view of the many WW II era buildings remaining on the field. Among the buildings are the chapel, base headquarters, and personnel building.

subjects such as code, radio procedure, tactics, and physical training; however, with the Japanese attack on Pearl Harbor on December 7, 1941, much of this would change. Earl Siddens still remembers when he first heard of the attack on Pearl Harbor. He was attending a movie in the Wilby Theater in downtown Selma when the movie was stopped, the announcement of the attack was made, and all military personnel were ordered to immediately return to the base. There, Earl was issued a 45 semi-automatic pistol, but with no ammunition because, as yet, he had not taken the required qualification course. He wondered what he was supposed to do with the pistol. The field was put on a seven-day work week, security increased, and the cadet blue uniform was changed to regulation khaki and olive drab. Training was accelerated to speed the flow of pilots into combat.

In November 1941, the first of many British cadets arrived at Craig Field for advanced training. For the next year and a half, Craig Field would see a steady flow of visitors from the United Kingdom. By the summer of 1943, when the program ended, 1,392 British cadets had earned their wings. Later, the French would train here, as well as a small number of Dutch. As mentioned, the first class to graduate did so in May 1941. This was a major event for the town of Selma and the surrounding region. Merchants ran ads in the local paper which supported the mayor's proclamation of the day as "Selma Flying Cadet Day." The ceremony which was held on the stage of the Wilby Theater in Selma on Thursday, May 29, was preceded with a parade down Broad Street. Cheered on by hundreds of citizens, the cadets were ushered into the theater where they heard an address and received their wings from Brigadier General Walter Weaver, commander of the Southeast Air Corps Training Center.

Most of the men flying the planes were low time pilots honing their skills in order to earn their wings. Accidents did happen, and probably the most common accident was the ground loop. It was caused by the pilot losing control of the aircraft after landing, and as a result the plane would go into a wide 180 degree turn on the ground. Sometimes the wing would dip, scrape the ground, and perhaps rip off a landing gear.

131

Reuben Bishop repaired lots of ground loop damage to the wing tips of the T-6's used by the cadets. He worked in the sheet metal shop until September 1942, and then left to join the Navy. He would return to Craig Field following the war and become foreman of the sheet metal shop.

From this small beginning, and despite the shortages of instructors and material, the school graduated increasingly larger pilot training classes. By the end of 1943, the new training field had graduated 4,471 new pilots. Of this total, 1,392 were British and ten were Dutch. The British training program came to a close with class 43B in February 1943. This was a emotional loss for the people of Selma because the British cadets were well liked. Earl Siddens remembers that one night while returning with a cadet from a party off the base, they were stopped by a police officer. The officer wondered why the British cadet's face was red. The cadet told him that it was often foggy in England, and he seldom saw the sun. He said that if the officer were from England, his face would be red too. The officer laughed and let them go.

The very few Dutch students were spread out among three American squadrons and received the same training. While many of the Dutch students spoke excellent English, the differences in language still caused problems from time to time. The few Dutch students contrasted with the large number of French students that began to arrive at Craig Field in early November 1943 for advanced flight training. Craig Field was selected by the Air Corps as the only field to give advanced single engine training and P-40 transition training to the French. Craig Field also gave training in the Martin B-26 Marauder. Many of these students had formally served in the French North African Army or had left France after the armistice and earned the opportunity to become pilots. At this time, Craig Field was also teaching fighter transition training using the Curtiss P-40.

During 1943, changes were made in the training program as a result of lessons learned both in training and from combat. A major training change, one that was to have a significant morale effect upon the cadets, was put into practice as a result of an Army Air Forces Flying Training Command memorandum dated May 19, 1943. In effect, it said that only 70% of the students would receive fixed gunnery training. These students were the ones "considered to be the best potential fighter pilots or potential advanced single-engine instructors." Those not among the 70% were to become "basic flying instructors, ferry pilots, and co-pilots for multi-engine aircraft." Several factors were to be considered in the decision as to who would get the gunnery training. These included, desire, proficiency in the theory of gunnery, and instructors' selection based upon pilot proficiency, and mental aptitude. The memo, which went into effect with class 43-F made clear who would have an opportunity to become a fighter pilot and who would not. Those falling into the 30% group typically went to non-fighter assignments. This caused problems, especially with those cadets selected for the 30% group. Fighter pilot selection had to be made early in the training, and as a

The chapel as it appeared during the war and as it is today. Today the chapel is used as a branch library for the City of Selma.

(USAF VIA OTHA CARNEAL, THE OLD DEPOT &THOLE)

opportunity to stay with their flying training at twin engine schools. Fifty-four students qualified under this program during 1943 and continued their training at Turner Field, George Field, Columbus Army Air Field, Blytheville Army Air Field, Freeman Field, and Stuttgart Field. The program did not prove to be satisfactory and was changed in January 1944.

By 1944, training was in full swing. A good example of this is the size of the group that graduated in January 1944. This class (44-A) graduated 226 trainees out of a class of 286. At the time, it was reported to be the largest class ever for the school. But, the newly commissioned officers and flight officers did not leave the field immediately after the ceremony. Bad weather had caused them to miss some flying training, and they were required to stay about 10 more days to finish. By this time, the school was also becoming more standardized. During 1943, the instruction program was changed in many areas as a result of the elimination of some courses and the addition of others. The first major effort toward standardization came in early 1943. At that time, the Southeast Flying Training Command issued a memo which covered all phases of flying and ground instruction. The memo stated that ground school for the advanced single-engine schools was to be a minimum of sixty hours of instruction; however, each school was allowed to give additional hours if necessary to bring each class up to a recognized standard of proficiency. By late 1944, Craig Field was involved in three major areas of training: Advanced-Single Engine pilot training, P-40 Transition training, and a Preflight Program for French students.

result, there was a constant shifting and reassignment of cadets from one group to another. In many cases, their ego was negatively affected by the selection of cadets for the non-fighter pilot group. Perhaps one reason for this change was the fact that there were too many cadets who wanted to become fighter pilots.

The seventy/thirty program hurt morale; however, one program that helped started in mid 1943 and was called "The Pilot Salvage Program." This initiative allowed some cadets who had been eliminated from the single engine schools, the

In addition to the men who arrived for pilot training, thousands more passed through Craig Field either as members of pre-flight cadet pools, or as part of the program known as "On-the-Line Trainees." Essentially both programs were the result of having too many men available for aircrew training at a time when the need was becoming less urgent. Probably, the first holding pool at Craig Field was established in December 1943 when 678 newly classified cadets and aviation students arrived from the Classification Center at Nashville, Tennessee. The intent was to keep them at Craig Field for a short time, and then send them on to pre-flight training at Maxwell Field. They received some training at Craig Field, but their real value was in doing menial tasks on the flight line and other areas of the field. This procedure relieved the personnel stationed at Craig for more demanding work. In January, a large number were transferred to Maxwell Field to begin pre-flight training; these were immediately replaced by hundreds more.

The more formal program of "On-the-Line Trainees" began in September 1944. Its stated purpose was to give training in the pre-cadet phase. In actuality, it was just a way to hold men in reserve until training facilities were available or the need became greater for replacement aircrews. It also helped to replace the permanent party personnel who were being siphoned from the training fields into ground combat. Each field was given broad latitude by Army Air Forces Headquarters in the training and use of these men. The instruction from headquarters was that "trainees will be given duty assignments with aircraft maintenance and servicing where they will get more practical training for their future instruction." As a result, their employ-

ment/training varied from base to base. Craig Field put together a structured training program for these visitors which was broken into three parts: administration, supply, and engineering. The trainees' schedules included classroom work and on the job training. When first established in September 1944, there were 601 men in the group. In general, the morale of the trainees was poor because they saw this program as just another delay in their plans to get into aviation.

A new program that started at Craig Field during 1944 was a Preflight school for French

MAIN ENTRANCE

Two photos of the main gate to Craig Field. One is the entrance during WW II and the other as it was in late 1996.

(USAF VIA GEORGE SWIFT, THE CROSSROADS & THOLE)

Post headquarters then and now. Today the building is used by the Craig Field Airport Authority. (USAF VIA GEORGE SWIFT, THE CROSSROADS & THOLE)

A late 1996 view of the former Post Office. The building next to it was the Post Exchange.

Scenes from the interior of the Post Exchange. (USAF VIA GEORGE SWIFT, THE CROSSROADS)

This T-33 is mounted on a pylon near the entrance to the field, and pays tribute to the members of the 29th Flying Training Wing who served at Craig Field. The plaque on the pylon reads: "29th FTW Served Here With Distinction, 1940–1977."

A SQUADRON BARRACK

A wartime view of a Squadron Barracks. (USAF VIA GEORGE SWIFT, THE CROSSROADS)

Two views of former barracks buildings as they were in late 1996.

students. This training was given to the students before they left for Primary Flight training or Flexible Gunnery training at Tyndall Field in Florida.

During 1945, the training activities at Craig Field continued, but the classes were smaller, because of the need for fewer pilots. The number of returned combat veterans on the field continued to increase, and in this group was a large number of pilots. The class that finished in early August, Class 45-E, contained just 63 graduates. When Class 45-G reported for advanced training on August 6, it had a total of 160 students. In this total were 56 French students. The war would end a few days later, and with it the training of American cadets. The

training of French students continued through 1945, and was ended in January 1946.

Following the war, the mission of Craig Field changed from time to time, but it remained primarily a training base. The Special Staff School was established here in June 1946, when it was transferred from Orlando, Florida. With the desperate need for additional pilots created by the Korean War, Craig Field was again placed in the pilot training business; this occurred in September 1950 when the 3615th Pilot Training Wing was established. The field's new mission was to give advanced conventional single engine training and pilot instructor training. In 1953, Craig Field stopped its basic single engine training and

137

Graduation day with the ceremonies held in the Pecan Grove. Typically when weather permitted graduation ceremonies were held out of doors in the Pecan Grove. This stand of trees was saved from destruction when the field was built. They are still on the field today.

(USAF VIA GEORGE SWIFT, THE CROSSROADS)

focused its efforts upon pilot instructor training. By 1976, Craig Field was an undergraduate pilot training base (UPT). The field was selected as one of two bases to be closed in an economy move. In 1977, Air Training Command closed Craig Field along with Webb Air Force Base in Texas. Craig Field graduated its last undergraduate pilot training class (77-08) on August 12, 1977. The 29th Flying Training Wing was inactivated on September 30, and the field was placed on caretaker status the next day.

Today, the former training field is Selma's municipal airport, and is called Craig Field Airport and Industrial Complex. As the name implies, it is a growing industrial park with major aviation facilities including an 8000-foot runway. It is home to many industries including the Raytheon Corporation which, among other things, refurbishes aircraft for the military.

Most of the former WW II structures remaining on Craig Field are in excellent condition. This building was the Base Personnel building.

138

PART OF CANTONMENT BARRACKS AREA

An overview picture of the barracks area that was taken early in the field's history. In the far left-hand corner can be seen the tops of the pyramidal tents, that at the time, were probably still being used to house soldiers.

(USAF VIA GEORGE SWIFT, THE CROSSROADS)

This is one of the hangars remaining from WWII and may have been the sub-depot hangar. It is now used by the Raytheon Corporation.

The former NCO Club building. This structure may have been built following the war.

B-29's on display at the base. The picture was probably taken at the end of the war.

(TERRY TURNER)

12

Combat Crew Training

Sioux City Army Air Base

The construction of Sioux City Army Air Base, located about six miles south of Sioux City, Iowa, began in March 1942, about three months after the Japanese attack on Pearl Harbor. The building program proceeded rapidly, so that by the following September, most of the major construction was finished. The runways were originally 6000 feet long; however, by October they had been lengthened to 8000 feet in order to accommodate the heavy bombers that would soon be landing at the base. Sioux City Army Air Base would train crew members of B-24's and B-17's, and at its peak, (October 1943) there were 940 officers and 5,183 enlisted men either assigned or attached to the base. The major training activities at Sioux City included aerial gunnery, bombardment, navigation, formation flying, and other related courses. Part of the new airfield was built on the already existing site of the Sioux City municipal airport. The former pas-

senger terminal building was converted into an officer's club, and another building was used for the civilian flights which continued out of the field during the war. An interesting side note is that former movie star Jimmy Stewart took training here with the 445th Bomb Group.

Of the early military personnel to arrive on the base, a group of 22 officers and enlisted men came in July 1942. These men were the advance party, and their job was to prepare the field for the thousands of soldiers who would follow. The field's first commanding officer was Major Eugene Cunningham who assumed this responsibility on July 5, 1942. At the time, the field was in the middle of construction, and the soldiers made do with what was available. Often they were forced to improvise using nail kegs and building material for office furniture. Since their were no barracks ready for occupation, the men stayed in a local hotel.

Over time, the important parts of the base were completed and put into service. An interesting look at how the base came together can be seen by reviewing the major events of its construction. One of the early requirements was to put in a railroad spur to effectively and quickly move men and material to the base. This rail-

An aerial view of the cantonment area of Sioux city Army Air Base. This photo was probably taken in 1945, perhaps later. Note the B-29's sitting on the ramp.

(USAF VIA TERRY TURNER)

road spur was completed in June with the connection to the main line made at the nearby community of Sergeant Bluff. To obtain drinking water, wells were completed in July, and by the end of September most of the roads were finished. A post office and a dispensary were located in the headquarters building as a temporary measure until the appropriate buildings were completed. The skeet and pistol range was finished in August about the same time as the Target Butt for testing the aircraft machine guns. The Base Headquarters was finished during April 1942. Living quarters, warehousing, and the hospital facilities were under construction by April, but were not completed until the end of November. The base hospital opened in October.

Some of the structures built to help improve the morale of the soldiers were the Recreational Hall, a theater (with a seating capacity for 1,038 people), and two chapels. By 1945, the east chapel was used for Protestant services and the west for Catholic services. The base theater opened officially in September with the first film being *Across the Pacific* starring Humphry Bogart. During the first year, the number of movies shown were increased from five per week to twenty-one. There were three viewings per day to accommodate the shift workers, and about 5000 tickets were sold each week. Also finished in August were two enlisted men's mess halls, the officer's mess hall, and a mess hall for 475 cadets. A school building was completed, along with the fire station, a Link Trainer building, and a building to safeguard the secret

Norden bombsight. The Control Tower opened in August at about the same time as the base guard house which had a capacity for 57 prisoners. Until early October 1942, the base was guarded by civilians. The runway system was quite extensive and required huge outlays of material. The runways, and their taxi strips, along with the drainage system were started during June. The first phase was finished in August; however, the extension (from 6000 feet to 8000 feet), began in September and was done by the end of October. Then as now, rumors about military waste made the news. The local paper reported in its September 18 edition that contractors were burning stockpiles of surplus lumber. Untrue, claimed the base executive officer, Major Malcolm Seashore, who said the lumber would be put to other uses such as building bookcases, etc.

Unlike many of the new "temporary" training bases built to meet the need for the rapid expansion of the Army Air Forces, there were many opportunities for off base entertainment for the men and women stationed at Sioux City. In addition to the theaters, restaurants, and night clubs in and around Sioux City, there were three USOs. Two of them were located in Sioux City, and the other in the nearby town of Sergeant Bluff. The one at Sergeant Bluff opened on October 15, 1942 and was the best equipped. The amenities included a large dance hall, equipped for movies, a snack bar, kitchen, showers, and meeting rooms. Like all the USOs it was supported by local churches and other organizations, who provided volunteers to help the sol-

This is a good photo of the six navigation training towers that were located just behind the hangars on the flight line. Parts of some of these buildings remain today in the town of Sergeant Bluff where they were converted into one story apartment buildings.

(BOB STOLZE)

A partial view of the ramp area. The T-6's indicate this photo was taken after the war. (BOB STOLZ)

Exchange, and do other acts of kindness for the patients. Their visits were something the GIs looked forward to; their visits helped to brighten the day.

One of the first nurses to report to the new base hospital during late 1942, was Mrs. Lillian Gondek. She had been a nurse in civilian life and along with a friend volunteered for nursing duty just after Pearl Harbor. After a short stay at Camp Crowder in Missouri for reassignment, Lillian now a second lieutenant was sent to the base. She did not know much about the base at Sioux City, and on the train ride there thought she was going to Sioux Falls, South Dakota, which at the time, had a large radio operator's school. She met her husband, Ted while working on the base, and they were later married in the Protestant Chapel. The chapel is still on the former base today.

Lillian remembers her basic military training as a "joke." To her, it seemed as though it was something that was belatedly thought up. The training started with her arrival at Sioux City Army Air Base, with perhaps a bit while she was at Camp Crowder. Her basic training at Sioux City, was in addition to her normal duties, and

diers, visit with them, and serve refreshments such as cookies, cake, soft drinks and coffee. Dances were held on a regular basis and were strictly chaperoned. Thousands of lonely soldiers, some about to leave for combat, spent many pleasant evenings at the USOs and were able to forget, at least for a while, their uncertain future.

A patriotic group, one of many who volunteered their time and effort at the air base, was the Grey Ladies, an auxiliary arm of the American Red Cross. There were about sixty active members in the Sioux City area, and they worked in the base hospital from around noon each day to about 4:00 p.m. Typically they would pass out writing materials, cigarettes, and visit with the sick or wounded soldiers. Often they would help write letters, run errands to the Postal

Today's view of the former cantonment area. Note the modern tower and the former WW II chapel located below the tower near the cluster of buildings in the center of the photo. (RICK ALTER AND TERRY TURNER)

144

consisted of two sessions per week from 5 A.M. to 6 A.M. There were no manuals or teaching aids. A Staff Sergeant told her that one of the most important lessons the new Army nurses needed to learn was how to properly salute their superiors.

There were three departments in the hospital, medical, surgical, and psychiatric, and the working shifts were generally eight hours, ie. 7 A.M. to 3 P.M., or 3 P.M. to 11 P.M., etc. Lillian recalls how the various hospital buildings were connected by long corridors so the patients could be moved from building to building, out of the weather. In the summer, the corridors were excessively hot and in winter, they tended to fill with the blowing snow that came in through the gaps in the wood framing and around the windows. On occasion, it was difficult to move a patient from one building to another because of the accumulation of snow on the floor of the corridor. Lillian still remembers with sadness the many training accidents, and the injured young men who were brought to the hospital.

By mid September 1942 the first phase of construction was finished and the field was opened for the public to see the newest Army Air Forces training field. This was a major event for the city and the *Sioux City Journal* reported in its September 17th edition "Air Base Tour Here Saturday." Movie stars including Ralph Bellamy, Richard Arlen, and Peggy Diggins would be at the base to sell bonds and stamps. Those who purchased a $25.00 war bond would be allowed to tour the base and see barracks, the mess hall, theater, hangars, control tower, and views of the runway. Unlike today, there was considerable patriotic involvement by the local citizens in the building of the base, and much of the furnishings in the recreations rooms (Day Rooms) for the squadrons were given by local groups, including, the

Two aerial views of the former training base as it appears today.
(RICK ALTER AND TERRY TURNER)

Quota Club, Kiwanis Club, Rotary Club, Lions Club, Saint Thomas Episcopal Church, First Presbyterian Church, First Christian Church, Jewish Federation, the Blessed Sacrament Church, the Junior League, Immaculate Conception Church, and the several First Lutheran Churches surrounding the air base. Items donated included couches, easy chairs, table, radios, writing tables, floor lamps, pictures, and curtains.

During 1943, training at the field was intended to prepare an entire bomb group for overseas combat. Later, after sufficient Bomb Groups had been formed and trained, the base switched to training individual crews as replacements or

This 1992 photo shows some of the former barracks that remain on the field today. With the exception of the chapel the few WW II buildings remaining are scheduled to be torn down.

A 1995 view of the last WW II hangar. It has since been removed. (TERRY TURNER)

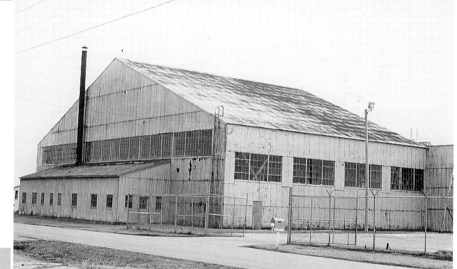

The former fire station as it was in 1992. During WW II, a B-17 crashed into the building.

A post war view of the front gate looking toward the flight line. The small sign by the chapel reads "Small Lot Sales."

(BOB STOLZ)

additions to various bomb groups. When Melvin Scott arrived at the field in May 1944, the training was well organized and delivered effectively. Melvin was a B-17 pilot and had been joined up with his crew at Lincoln Army Air Field in Lincoln, Nebraska. After finishing crew training, they would leave for combat over Europe. He would later fly 35 missions with the 334th Squadron of the 95th Bomb Group.

He recalls at the time there were about 40 B-17's, F and G models in use at the time. These were not war wearies, but ships in good condition with some of the G models relatively new. Melvin's training included both ground and air work. The ground subjects included weather, code, ship and aircraft identification, aircraft systems, and navigation. The air work was intensive. He flew about 158 hours with formation flying, bombing, and gunnery as part of the curriculum. He recalls very few, if any, high altitude missions

that went much more than 18,000 feet. This was probably a function of their complexity, ie. oxygen requirements, problems with equipment performance at the extreme low temperatures at altitude, and the low octane gas which hampered performance. This was fine with Melvin because he did not like flying at these altitudes. Later in Europe, he became used to it because so many of the missions were flown at

One of the base chapels that still remains on the field today.

147

This was a former mess hall as it appeared during the author's visit in 1992. The building has since been removed.

A view of building 801 which was used as a shop for welding, sheet metal work, prop repair, paint work and shipping and receiving. The building has since been torn down.

Some warehouse buildings which may have been removed after the photo was taken in 1992.

a high altitude. While at Sioux City, he did a lot of formation flying. The largest group was a squadron (12 planes); however, most of the practice was in smaller groups of about four aircraft. This was difficult flying, and the key was to anticipate what your leader or wingman was going to do. This helped to eliminate abrupt throttle movements, saving gas and engine wear. Some of his formation flying included trips to Davenport, Iowa and Brunning, Nebraska. The saying often heard by the pilot while practicing was "Get it up there" or "Get it in tight." Melvin feels this was one of the hardest lessons he had to learn while flying the B-17. He did not like night formation flying because of the problems associated with vertigo. This was especially a concern in bad weather when he had to shift his focus from the instruments to checking the plane's position in the formation. Also, the cloud formations could play havoc with a pilot's sense of attitude. Over time, with training and experience, he became better at it and was comfortable with this type of flying.

Mrs. Lillian Gondek and her husband during their marriage ceremony in the Protestant Chapel. Mrs. Gondek was a nurse assigned to the base hospital. Her husband was also assigned to the base. The chapel is still on the former base.
(GONDEK)

Floyd "Casey" Clark was a belly turret gunner who took his training at Sioux City during December/March 1944/45. He remembers the cold weather, and how nice it was not to hear the squeaking of brakes and engines being run up in the morning. This meant bad weather, giving him a chance to sleep longer that morning.

Training was not without risks; many young men would die in training accidents before they had an opportunity to be tested in combat. The first lives that were lost at Sioux City Army Air Base in an aircraft accident happened on October 4, 1942 when two crewman were killed. Just two months later another ten men died in a crash of a B-17 in a field near the base during a snowstorm. The B-17 was a fine aircraft, one of the very best for its day; however, learning to operate it was not without risk. During World War II, there were about 1,600 aircraft accidents with the B-17 in the continental United States, about 480 of the planes were wrecked, and approximately 1,760 men lost their lives.

The 307th Bomb Group arrived on September 29, 1942 and was the first group to start training at Sioux City. Later, the group left on October 19 for duty in the South Pacific. They were followed by the 100th Bomb Group that

arrived in late December. Other groups trained here included, the 99th, the 379th, the 384th, the 445th, and the 448th. During 1943, there were about 28 B-17's assigned to the base. This number must have increased significantly because a report dated April 1945 talked about a formation flight of sixty "TB-17's."

During World War II, the quality and length of training the airman received depended upon the point in the war that the airman received his training. In early 1942, facilities were just being built, there were few training aids, no standardized training programs, and few trained instructors. Many airmen reported to their assigned base with little or no basic training. Men were desperately needed to assume a combat role immediately, so each training field did the best it could with very limited facilities and supplies. Improvisation was the way to get things done and a high premium was placed upon individual initiative and imagination. Sioux City was no exception.

A couple of newspaper articles give the reader a good idea of the training progress during the war. The first article talks about the improvement in gun turret training, and was published in the May 1944 edition of the base newspaper, *The Flying Sioux*. This was about one year before the

Lt. Melvin Scott second from the left, front row, and his crew with their B-17 in England. Mr. Scott flew 35 missions during WW II and earned the Distinguished Flying Cross. Later, at age 47, he would fly in Vietnam as a transport pilot. Mr. Scott retired as a Lt. Colonel and in 1998 was inducted in the South Dakota Aviation Hall of Fame. (MELVIN SCOTT)

end of the war in Europe, and almost two and a half years after the start of the war. The article said " . . . One of the best turret schools in the Second Air Force is now in operation here at Sioux City. Under M/Sgt Mahlon Leed, a competent staff of instructors, all combat veterans and specialists in their respective fields, pass on the experience they have gained to future B-17 combat crewmen. The well-equipped school is a far cry from the school established a few months ago with only three turrets. Since it moved into Building 906, the turret school has equipped itself with all the armaments carried by B-17 F's and G's, Sperry upper, Sperry lower ball and Bendix chin turrets. Now that renovation of building 906 has been completed (all done by instructors during their time off from classes), a number of class rooms are available with five turrets in each. It is possible to accommodate any number of students on a 12-hour schedule each day."

Gunnery training also was practiced in the air. Melvin Scott's crew practiced both air to air and air to ground training. The air to ground training was practiced along the Missouri River near the Nebraska border where silhouettes and bulls eye targets were set up along the river banks. For this type of practice mission, the aircraft flew around 400 to 500 feet above the ground while the gunners fired at the targets. The rumor was that this practice was in anticipation of supporting ground troops in battle by strafing enemy positions. Melvin also fired all the B-17's guns, with the exception of the belly gun, while the plane was in flight.

Another article published earlier in the base newspaper during September 1943 talked about a new navigation training device, a Celestial Trainer: ". . . According to Edwin Link who also invented the ingenious Link Trainer, the synthetic devices of the celestial trainer simulate actual fly-

When this picture was taken (late '44, early '45 at Sioux City Army Air Base) Floyd Clark was a ball turret gunner in a B-17. Floyd is in the middle of the front row. Following his B-17 training at Sioux City, Floyd was sent to Pyote Army Air Field for further training in B-29's. He had orders for the South Pacific, but they were canceled when the war with Japan ended. (FLOYD CLARK)

ing conditions—any weather, day or night by instruments, radio and the stars. Primarily, the Celestial Trainer was adapted for the use of navigators, although pilots, co-pilots, and radio operators find this group of devices very helpful. By means of the artificial stars set in the revolving dome, the navigator is at all times sure of his course and position. In the Celestial Trainer, the pilot and co-pilot are flying by instrument. Whereas the original Link Trainer had room for only one man, the Celestial Trainer accommodates four men whose duties are closely interrelated in flying. The radio operator is in constant contact with the man in the control room. The man in the control room is familiar with their flight problems and he sits in judgment of their ability and knowledge."

The Celestial Trainers were quite advanced for their day and were contained in an air-conditioned octagonal shaped building several stories high. In addition to the overhead display of a rotating dome of stars to help guide the navigators, there was also a screen below the trainee's platform that projected moving terrain. Typically, the training crew was made up of the pilot, co-pilot, navigator, and radio operator. The trainers first went into operation at Sioux City in 1943.

The new crews also practiced navigation while in the air. Melvin Scott's new navigator became lost on his first night navigation mission. Their assignment was to fly from Sioux City to Hutchinson, Kansas. The crew was fortunate that Melvin had kept track of the aircraft's

151

progress over the ground because after the navigator had passed Hutchinson and was not aware of it, Melvin was able to pinpoint his position. Over time, the navigator learned his lessons well and became a valuable member of the crew.

The historical report of the 393rd Combat Crew Training School in February 1944 talked about another training improvement: "In order that combat crews in training at this station become familiar with general living and working conditions in that area where they will ultimately be based, the Sioux City Air Base has created a theater-of-war atmosphere. Instructions from the 46th Bombardment Operational Wing have been followed to the letter and the change over from Sioux City to "Ipswich" has been brought out in every detail. The names of English coast towns, as well as a few inland towns has been put on the street signs in the combat training area—names such as Eastbourne, Great Yarmouth, and Dungeness Road, which the men, if based at Ipswich, would be most likely to see from the air as they depart and return from combat missions. To carry the illusion a little further, the combat mess hall is now labeled 'Airman's Mess,' same as in England."

The training of B-17 crews continued until the war in Europe was over. Around that time, the field received a new mission which required the conversion of the facilities for B-29 training. The base was transferred to the 17th Bombardment Operational Training Wing and began the transition to start B-29 training. By early June, there were ten B-29's on the field. The new training program was short lived, however; because in August 1945 it was canceled. With the end of World War II, the former training base switched from training men to processing them out of the service and back into civilian life. This was Sioux City's Army Air Base's final role in WW II. This was a happier time, when more than 12,000 officers and enlisted men were processed through the base at war's end. The last one separated from the service on December 1, and the base closed in December 1945. It was not idle long, however, because in August, part of the base was again in use by an air reserve unit, and later by the Iowa National Guard.

Commanders of the field during the WW II period were: Lt. Col. Eugene Cunningham, Major Charles Trowbridge, Col. John Eaton, Col. George Blakey, (he served as base commander during three different periods), Col. Wallace Dawson, Col. Downs Ingram, Lt. Col. William Calhoun, and Col. Marion Munn (who assumed command during October 1945).

Today, the field still serves as the municipal airport for the metro area surrounding Sioux City, known locally as "Siouxland." The airport is named the Sioux Gateway Airport. As recently as 1992, there were several WW II structures remaining on the field, but over time, many have been torn down. One of the WW II buildings still remaining is the former civilian passengers' terminal. This building along with five other former WW II structures houses the Mid America Air Museum. The museum's display building is the former civilian terminal building. This is a temporary location as the museum has plans to build a new facility on 25 acres near its current location.

The field continues to retain its military involvement with units of the 185th Fighter Wing of the Iowa National Guard flying F-16's from the field's 15,602 foot runway. The guard unit has a prestigious history of service at Sioux City that dates back to 1946. One of the commanders was Col. Dennis Swanstrom, who retired in late 1998. The unit has taken part in the Korean War, Vietnam, and northern Iraq in 1993 and 1996. In Vietnam the unit flew thousands of combat hours and lost one pilot to combat (1st Lt. Warren Brown). The 174th Tactical Fighter Squadron, the flying squadron of the 185th Wing, flew more combat sorties than any other Air National Guard unit involved in the Vietnam War. Among other awards, the unit was awarded the Presidential Unit Citation. This is a proud unit that has won the Spaatz trophy (1956 and 1990) recognizing it as the best Air Guard unit in the country. In addition, the unit has been awarded the Air Force Outstanding Unit award four times.

**This section has several items of interest that
relate to flying activities during WW II.**

On the left is Horace Dimond's *White Instrument* card dated June 3, 1941, and on the right his *Pilot Identification*
card dated March 23, 1940.

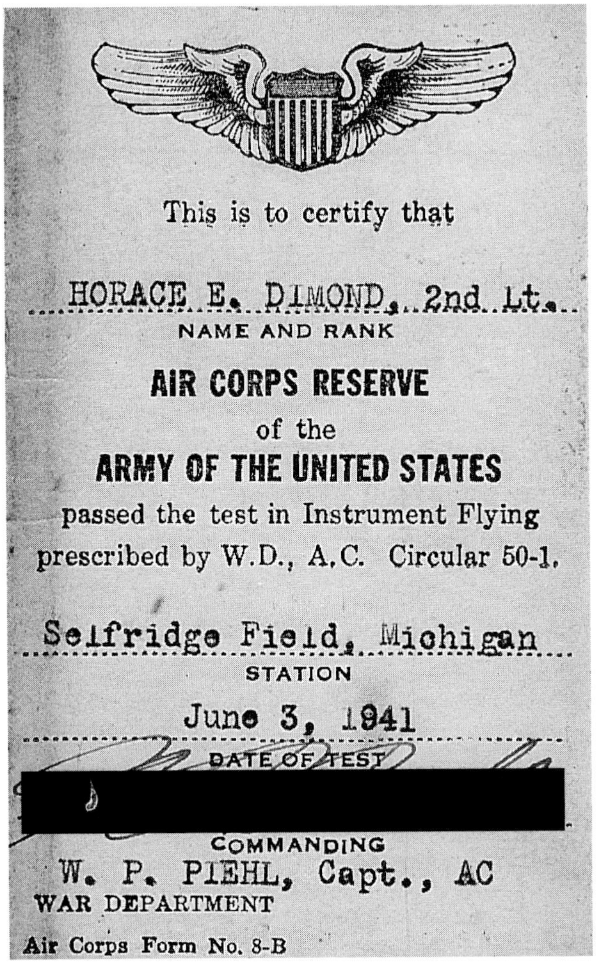

This is to certify that

HORACE E. DIMOND, 2nd Lt.
NAME AND RANK

AIR CORPS RESERVE
of the
ARMY OF THE UNITED STATES

passed the test in Instrument Flying
prescribed by W.D., A.C. Circular 50-1,

Selfridge Field, Michigan
STATION

June 3, 1941
DATE OF TEST

COMMANDING
W. P. PIEHL, Capt., AC
WAR DEPARTMENT

Air Corps Form No. 8-B

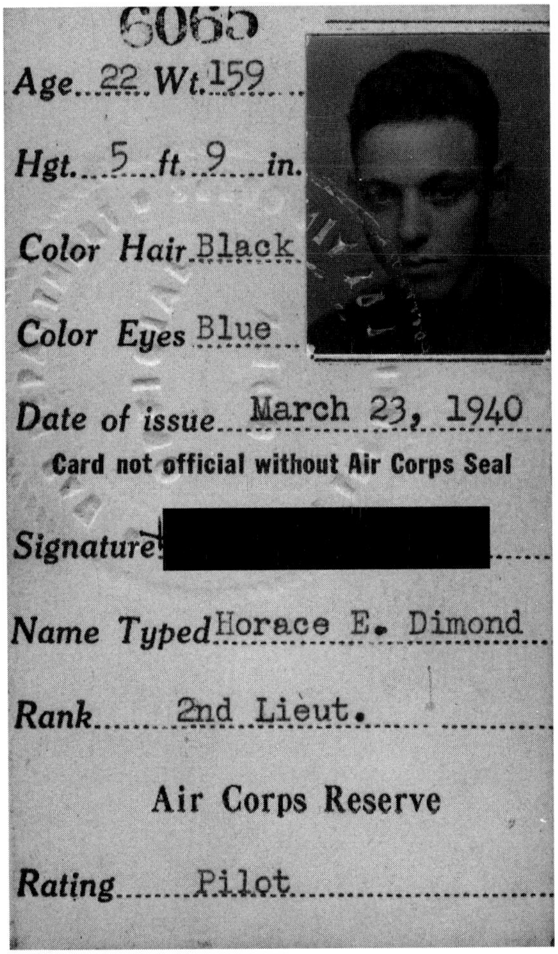

6065

Age 22 Wt. 159

Hgt. 5 ft. 9 in.

Color Hair Black

Color Eyes Blue

Date of issue March 23, 1940

Card not official without Air Corps Seal

Signature

Name Typed Horace E. Dimond

Rank 2nd Lieut.

Air Corps Reserve

Rating Pilot

Lt. Anthony Kretten. This photo may have been taken while he was
on leave following pilot training.   (KRETTEN)

Right: *Form 5—Individual Flight Record for Anthony (Tony) Kretten,
August 1945, 4th Combat Cargo Group.*

Mr. Kretten's Form 5 lists his total combat time as a little more than
765 hours which includes 438 combat missions. This was dangerous
flying because of the primitive nature of the airfields and facilities,
possible interception by Japanese fighters, and the altitude required
to fly the heavily loaded C-46 over the mountains.
    Many of Mr. Kretten's flights were in support of the British
campaign against the Japanese in Burma. Often he flew into dirt
strips, and on at least one occasion, had to circle the strip waiting for
the battle to end before he was able to land the plane. He recalls
hauling just about anything on these missions including food, ammo,
cement, British beer, and fresh mutton. He recalls: "We were all truck
drivers. I got to know Burma as well as my hometown. "

WAR DEPARTMENT
AAF FORM NO. 5
APPROVED DEC. 7, 1942

INDIVIDUAL FLIGHT RECORD

(1) SERIAL NO. 0-710 483 (2) NAME KRETTEN ANTHONY J (3) RANK 1st Lt (4) AGE 1920
                                   FIRST   MIDDLE
(5) PERS. CLASS 18 (6) BRANCH AAF (7) STATION APO 216, New York
                                                           ATTACHED FOR FLYING
(8) ORGANIZATION ASSIGNED AAFIBT 14th C C Sqdn, 4th C C Gp
                          AIR FORCE   COMMAND   WING   GROUP   SQUADRON   DETACHMENT
(9) ORGANIZATION ATTACHED _____ AIRFORCE ___ COMMAND ___ WING ___ GROUP ___ SQUADRON ___ DETACHMENT Same as 10
(10) PRESENT RATING & DATE Pilot 8 Feb 1944 (11) ORIGINAL RATING & DATE None
(12) TRANSFERRED FROM _____ (13) FLIGHT RESTRICTIONS None
(15) TRANSFERRED TO _____ (14) TRANSFER DATE _____

DO NOT WRITE IN THIS SPACE

(16)

PERS CLASS	RANK	RTG.	A. F.	COMMAND	WING	GROUP NO.	GROUP TYPE	SQUADRON NO.	SQUADRON TYPE	STATION	MO.	YR.	(17) MONTH August 19 4
:		:	: :	: :	: :	: :	: :	: :	: :	: : :			

DAY	AIRCRAFT TYPE, MODEL & SERIES	NO. LANDINGS	FLYING INST. (INCL. IN 1ST PIL. TIME) S	COMMD. PILOT C CA	CO-PILOT CP	QUALI-FIED PILOT DUAL QD	FIRST PILOT DAY P	FIRST PILOT NIGHT P N OR NI	RATED PERS. NON-PILOT P-AI			NON-RATED OTHER ARMS & SERVICES	NON-RATED OTHER (CREW) & PASS'GR	SPECIAL INFORMATION INSTRU-MENT I	SPECIAL INFORMATION NIGHT N	SPECIAL INFORMATION INSTRU-MENT TRAINER	PILOT NON-MIL. AIRCRAFT OVER 400 H.P.	PILOT NON-MIL. AIRCRAFT UNDER 400 H.P.
18	19	20	21	22	23	24	25	26	27	28	29	30	31	32	33	34	35	36
10	C-46D	1			4:00													
11	C-46D	1			4:00													
12	C-46D	1					3:35											
14	C-46D	2			3:50		4:25											
18	C-46D	2			2:45		2:45		:30					:30	1:00			
22	C-46D	2			3:00		:45	2:15								4:30		
26	C-46D	1			1:00		1:00											
28	C-6	1			2:00		2:00		:25					:25	:50			
27	C-46D	1			1:35		:30	1:05								2:10		
30	C-46D	2					5:45											

CERTIFIED CORRECT: ▮▮▮▮▮▮▮▮▮▮

THOMAS G FLYNN JR
Captain, Air Corps
Ass't Operations Officer

		14																
COLUMN TOTALS					22:10		20:45	3:20	:55					:55	1:50	6:40		

	(42) TOTAL STUDENT PILOT TIME	(43) TOTAL FIRST PILOT TIME		(44) TOTAL PILOT TIME	
(37) THIS MONTH		24:05	:55	46:15	:55
(38) PREVIOUS MONTHS THIS F. Y.		37:25	3:40	78:10	3:35
(39) THIS FISCAL YEAR		61:30	4:35	124:25	4:30
(40) PREVIOUS FISCAL YEARS	250:05	359:40	7:05	1388:10	15:25
(41) TO DATE	250:05	421:10	11:40	1512:35	19:55

AIRCRAFT	NL			CARD NO. 1				CARD NO. 2					CARD NO. 3				
19	20	21	22	23	24	25	26	27	28	29	30	31	32	33	34	35	36

DO NOT WRITE IN THIS SPACE

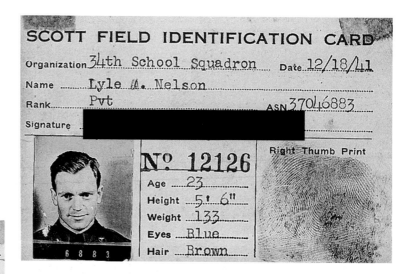

SCOTT FIELD IDENTIFICATION CARD

Organization 34th School Squadron   Date 12/18/41

Name ...... Lyle A. Nelson

Rank...... Pvt   ASN 37046883

Signature ▮▮▮▮▮▮▮▮▮▮

№ 12126

Age 23

Height ..5.ʹ 6.ʺ

Weight ..133

Eyes ....Blue

Hair ....Brown

Right Thumb Print

6 8 8 3

No. GC 15801   (a)

Age 24 .. Wt. 140 .

Hgt. 5 . ft. 6 . in.

Color Hair Brown.

Color Eyes Blue..

NELSON L A

5678   42 15 14

Date of issue .... 12-17-42 ..

Card not official without
Army Air Forces Seal

Signature . ▮▮▮▮▮▮▮▮

Name Typed Lyle.A..Nelson...

Rank...Second .Lieutenant...

ARMY AIR FORCES RESERVE

Aerial Observer (Navigator)
Rating.....................

Lyle Nelson's *Aerial Observer (Navigator) identification card* dated December 17, 1942, and his *Scott Field Identification card*.

Right: Lyle Nelson's *Officer's Pay Data Card*.

OFFICER'S PAY DATA CARD

Lyle A. Nelson, 2nd Lt. AC   O-669094

(Name)   (Serial number)   (Grade and arm or service)

Over ___0___ years' service   1st   pay period ____ years completed .... 19....

Monthly base pay and longevity .... $ 150.00

Additional pay for 75.00

Rental allowances 60.00

Subsistence ....30 day month 42.00

Date May 21, 1943   Total $ 327.00

Dependents: (State names and addresses)

-Wife-   Ruth Anna Neal Nelson
              Clarion, Iowa

Evidence of dependency (mother) filed with voucher No. .... 19 ....

Accounts of ....

Allotments class E $ .... $ .... $ ...

Insurance class D $ .... class N $ 6.70

Pay reservations class A $ ...

Other deductions $ ...

Subsequent changes in above data with dates thereof:

Last paid to include May 31, 1943
May, 1943 Accts. of D. S. COMBS, Major, FD.

(Changes affecting pay will be entered here and maintained up to date.

W. D., A. G. O. Form No 77
March 26 1942

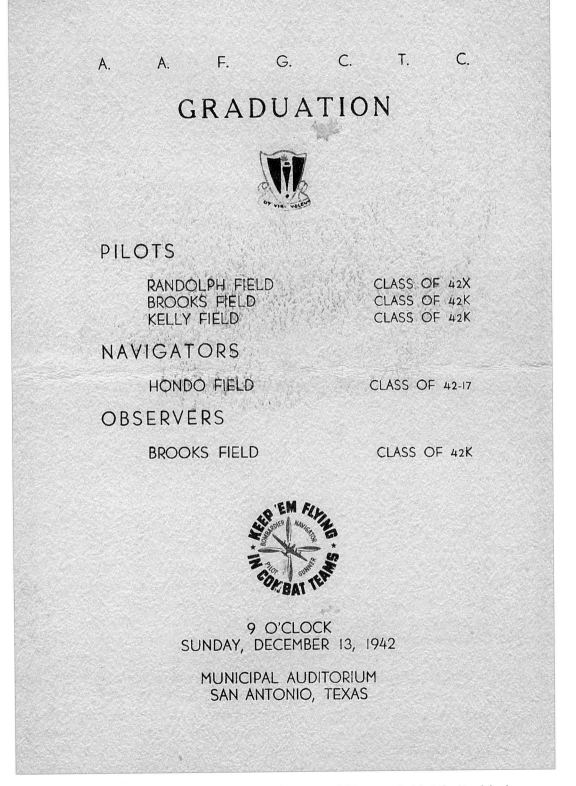

A. A. F. G. C. T. C.

GRADUATION

PILOTS

    RANDOLPH FIELD   CLASS OF 42X
    BROOKS FIELD   CLASS OF 42K
    KELLY FIELD   CLASS OF 42K

NAVIGATORS

    HONDO FIELD   CLASS OF 42-17

OBSERVERS

    BROOKS FIELD   CLASS OF 42K

9 O'CLOCK
SUNDAY, DECEMBER 13, 1942

MUNICIPAL AUDITORIUM
SAN ANTONIO, TEXAS

Front cover of a *graduation program* for Pilots, Navigators, and Observers held at the Municipal Auditorium, San Antonio, Texas, December 13, 1942. Guest speakers included Major General Barton Yount, and Lt. General Henry Arnold. (COURTESY OF LYLE NELSON)

157

Appendix II:
The Cocooning Project of Pyote AAF

The cocooning of the B-29's at Pyote, likely started in the early part of 1948 and was intended to preserve 601 B-29's. This number was probably reduced at a later date. The procedure described below is as described in the history of Pyote AAF, roll # B-2481. The film is available from the Air Force Historical Research Agency, Maxwell AFB, Alabama.

"After all corrosion has been treated, the aircraft is parked in its permanent place in the cocooning area. It is set on wooden blocks, moored and grounded. Final maintenance work is accomplished and the aircraft is turned over to the cocooning contractor. The first step is to spray a paint remover over the external black paint. After a few minutes, high-pressure water is used to remove the paint. At least 95% of the paint must be removed. The aircraft is then cleaned;

first; with steam containing a percentage of "formula C" cleaning compound, then with water under pressure. Next, it is inspected for external corrosion. If any is found it is treated. No zinc chromate paint can be used on surfaces so treated.

The following parts are removed: nose wheel and main gear nacelle doors, fairing of tail skid assembly, micro switches, airspeed indicators, pressure and static drain lines. Exposed openings are sealed and loose ends of micro switch wiring are taped up. Two inspection doors are removed from the bottom side and one from each wing tip, for the later installation of silica jell dehydrating agent.

In the next major operation, all openings, such as wheel wells, engine nose section, etc. are bridged with masking tape and the opening is sealed with a plastic web. Sealing compound is applied around these openings. All fabric and plexiglass surfaces are covered with scrin foil since the solvent in the cocooning plastic is very detrimental to

These photos were taken from the USAF micro film history of Pyote Army Air Field and are not good quality. However, they do provide a look at some parts of the cocooning process.

This worker appears to be either washing the aircraft or applying a protective coat.

A closer view of an engine during the cocooning process. The caption at the bottom of the picture reads "Yellow surface shows taping and webbing."

Left and below: Some of the homemade scaffolding that was built to help cocooning the B-29's.

these surfaces. Since the plastic will not adhere to metal a sealing compound is used on all vertical and hanging surfaces, such as lower half of the fuselage, bottom and leading edge of wings, horizontal stabilizer, etc.

The first coat of plastic is then applied. This coating is colored yellow. The yellow dye is added in order to aid mechanics and inspectors in checking the thickness and coverage. The yellow coat is applied in a cross-spray motion to provide competed coverage. The plastic is applied by starting at the highest point on the vertical stabilizer and working down and forward. After completion, the plastic is cut with a hole 8" long at each wheel nacelle and supercharge tailpipe. The purpose of this hole is to vent the aircraft. The yellow coat is inspected and all discrepancies corrected before application of the red plastic coat.

The second coat of plastic is then applied. This coat is colored red, and is applied in the same manner as the first. After completion of this step, the aircraft is dried out by using heaters. This is necessary due to condensation that takes place during spray operations, and to help remove solvent vapors present. 1500 lbs of dehydrating agent are then distributed throughout the aircraft. A total of six indicators are used in each airplane.

A plexiglass inspection window 10"×10" is installed in each engine in such a manner that the humidity indicator may be read. All openings in the cocoon are sealed and allowed to dry.

When the red coat has throughly dried, the Insul-matic (an asphalt type material) is then applied. This is sprayed on all vertical and hanging surfaces to a depth of 1/16". After this has been inspected and passed, an aluminum top coat is applied to upper half of the aircraft. This coating is applied to the upper half only due to lack of aluminum paint at this base. The purpose of this top coat is to reflect heat rays of the sun. The contractor then stencils the airplane serial number, type, model and series on the nose section.

After this covering has cured, the aircraft is turned over to the Procurement Inspection Section for final inspection and acceptance. A three-day inspection period is allowed. The humidity and temperature are checked daily. If the humidity exceeds 30%, the affected part is opened up and the spent dehydrating agent is removed and replaced with fresh. The aircraft is inspected for oil pockets, moisture pockets, ballooning, and damage to sealed joints. All damage is repaired by the contractor prior to acceptance of the completed cocooned aircraft."

Appendix III: USAAF Airfields

FIELD OR AIRSTRIP	MILES FROM NEAREST TOWN	FIELD OR AIRSTRIP	MILES FROM NEAREST TOWN
ALABAMA		Earnest Love Field	8 mi. NNE Prescott
		Luke Field	15 mi. WSW Phoenix
Anniston Army Air Field	15 mi. SW Anniston	Laguna Landing Strip	6 mi. NE Laguna
Auburn-Opelika	3 mi. E Auburn	McNeal aux. #1 (Douglas AAF, aux.)	Douglas
Autaugaville (Craig Field, aux.)	20 mi. W Selma	Marana Army Air Field	8 mi. NW Marana
Bates Field (ASC)	10 mi. W Mobile	Safford Field	6 mi. ENE Safford
Birmingham Army Air Field	5 mi. NE Birmingham	Sahuarita Flight Strip	2 mi. E Sahuarita
Brockley Field (ASC)	4 mi. S Mobile	Sky Harbor Airport (ATC)	2 mi. E Phoenix
Camp Sibert Army Air Field	3 mi. S Attala	Tucson Municipal Airport	6 mi. S Tucson
Courtland Army Air Field	1 mi. SW Courtland	Williams Field	9 mi. E Chandler
Craig Field	5 mi. SE Selma	Winslow Municipal Airport (ATC)	2 mi. SW Winslow
Dannelly Field	8 mi. SW Montgomery	Yucca Army Air Field	1 mi. NE Yucca
Demopolis Airfield (Key Field, aux.)	8 mi. WSW Demopolis	Yuma Army Air Field	2 mi. S Yuma
Dothan	2 mi. WNW Dothan		
Elmore (Gunter Field, aux.)	10 mi. N Montgomery	**ARKANSAS**	
Furniss (Craig Field, aux.)	10 mi. SSW Selma		
Gunter Field	2 mi. NE Montgomery	Adams Field (ATC)	2 mi. SE Little Rock
Henderson (Craig Field, aux.)	29 mi. SW Selma	Blytheville Army Air Field	2 mi. NW Blytheville
Huntsville Arsenal Field	7 mi. SW Huntsville	Carlisle (Stuttgart AAF, aux.)	26 mi. NW Stuttgart
Maxwell Field	2 mi. W Montgomery	Cooter (Blytheville AAF, aux.)	10 mi. NE Blytheville
Mollette (Craig Field, aux.)	16 mi. SSW Selma	Hazen (Stuttgart AAF, aux.)	19 mi. NNW Stuttgart
Muscle Shoals	1 mi. E Muscle Shoals	Hope Army Air Field	3 mi. NE Hope
Napier Field	7 mi. NW Dothan	Manila (Blytheville AAF, aux.)	13 mi. W Blytheville
Ozark Army Air Field	12 mi. SSW Ozark	Newport Army Air Field	6 mi. NE Newport
Roberts (Gliders only)	8 mi. NNW Birmingham	Praireville (Stuttgart AAF, aux.)	8 mi. SE Stuttgart
Selfield Field	4 mi. ENE Selma	Steele (Blytheville, AAF, aux.)	12 mi. N Blytheville
St. Elmo Municipal Airport (ASC)	St. Elmo	Stuttgart Army Air Field	6 mi. N Stuttgart
Tuskegee Army Air Field	7 mi. NW Tuskegee	Walnut Ridge Army Air Base	4 mi. NE Walnut Ridge
Tuskegee Institute #1	4 mi. SSE Tuskegee		
Tuskegee Institute #2	3 mi. N Tuskegee	**CALIFORNIA**	
ARIZONA		Allen (Gardner Field aux.)	25 mi. SE Taft
		Bakersfield Municipal Airport	4 mi. NW Bakersfield
Ajo Army Air Field	6 mi. N Ajo	Banning Landing Strip	1 mi. SE Banning
Coolidge Army Air Field	7 mi. SE Coolidge	Bidwell Field	2 mi. SW Red Bluff
Datelan Army Air Field	2 mi. NE Datelan	Bishop Army Air Field	2 mi. NE Bishop
Davis-Monthan Field	4 mi. SE Tucson	Blythe Army Air Field	7 mi. W Blythe
Douglas Army Air Field	8 mi. NNW Douglas	Camp Kearney NAAS	9 mi. N San Diego
Forrest aux. #2 (Douglas AAF, aux.)	6 mi. WNW Douglas	Chico Army Air Field	5 mi. NE Chico
Gila Bend Army Air Field	4 mi. S Gila Bend	Clover Field	3 mi. E Santa Monica
Gila Bend aux. #1	15 mi. SW Gila Bend	Concord Army Air Field	1 mi. NW Concord
Gila Bend aux. #2	18 mi. SSW Gila Bend	Daggett Municipal Airport	6 mi. E Daggett
Gila Bend aux. #3	8 mi. WSW Gila Bend	Delano Army Air Field	1 mi. S Delano
Hereford Army Air Field	1 mi. WNW Hereford	Desert Center Army Air Field	2 mi. NE Desert Center
Kingman Army Air Field	3 mi. NE Kingman		

161

FIELD OR AIRSTRIP	MILES FROM NEAREST TOWN	FIELD OR AIRSTRIP	MILES FROM NEAREST TOWN
Eagle Field	6 mi. SW Dos Palos	San Nicolas Army Air Field	75 mi. SW Los Angeles
Estrella Army Air Field	5 mi. NE Paso Robles	Santa Maria Army Air Field	4 mi. S Santa Maria
Eureka Navy Airport	14 mi. N Eureka	Santa Rosa Army Air Field	7 mi. NW Santa Rosa
Fairfield-Suisun Army Air Field	5 mi. E Fairfield	Shaver's Summitt Field	30 mi. ESE Indio
Gardner Field	8 mi. E Gardner	Siskiyou County Field	5 mi. NE Montaque
Grand Central Air Terminal		Stockton Field	4 mi. SSE Stockton
(March Field, sub base)	6 mi. NW Glendale	Thermal Army Air Field	2 mi. SW Thermal
Half Moon Bay Flight Strip	5 mi. NW Half Moon Bay	Victorville Army Air Field	5 mi. NW Victorville
Hamilton Field	7 mi. NNE San Rafiel	Visalia Army Air Field	6 mi. W Visalia
Hammer Field	5 mi. NE Fresno	Willows Airfield	
Hayward Army Air Field	3 mi. W Hayward	(Hamilton Field, aux.)	1 mi. W Willows
Hawthorne Field	1 mi. E Hawthorne	Winters Flight Strip	7 mi. NE Winters
Kern (Gardner Field, aux.)	21 mi. SE Taft	Van Nuys Metro Airport	17 mi. NW Los Angeles
Kern County Field	1 mi. WNW Inyokern		
Kern County Field	5 mi. NNW Bakersfield		
Kearney-Mesa Airport	8 mi. NE San Diego	COLORADO	
King City Field	2 mi. NNE King City		
Lemoore Army Air Field	9 mi. SW Lemoore	Arlington (La Junta, aux.)	28 mi. NNE Arlington
Lindbergh	2 mi. W San Diego	Buckley Field	8 mi. SE Denver
Lomita Flight Strip	1 mi. W Lomita	Denver Municipal Airport	5 mi. ENE Denver
Long Beach Army Air Field (ATC)	4 mi. NE Long Beach	La Junta Army Air Field	4 mi. NNE La Junta
Los Angeles Field	11 mi. SW Los Angeles	Las Animas (La Junta, aux.)	19 mi. NE La Junta
Lost Hills-Kern County	1 mi. NE Lost Hills	Leadville Flight Strip	2 mi. W Leadville
March Field	10 mi. SE Riverside	Lowry Field	1 mi. SE Denver
Marysville Army Air Field	3 mi. S Marysville	Peterson Field	7 mi. ESE Colorado
Mather Field	10 mi. E Sacramento		Springs
M C Flight Test Base	20 mi. SE Mojave	Pueblo Army Air Base	7 mi. ENE Pueblo
McClellan Field	8 mi. NE Sacramento	Pueblo Field	2 mi. SW Pueblo
Merced Army Air Field	6 mi. NW Merced	Rocky Ford (La Junta, aux.)	14 mi. NW La Junta
Merced Air Base (Merced AAF, aux.)	2 mi. NW Merced		
Metropolitan Airport	2 mi. NW Van Nuys		
Mills Field	10 mi. S San Francisco	CONNECTICUT	
Mines Field	10 mi. SW Los Angeles		
Minter Field	14 mi. NW Bakersfield	Bradley Field	2 mi. W Windsor Locks
Modesto Field	2 mi. ESE Modesto	Brainard Field	2 mi. SSE Hartford
Montague Airfield	3 mi. NE Montague	Bridgeport Army Air Field	3 mi. SE Stratford
Muroc Army Air Field	1 mi. S Muroc	Groton Army Air Field	3 mi. SE Groton
Muroc Flight Test Base	3 mi. N Muroc	New Haven Army Air Field	3 mi. SE New Haven
Napa Airfield	5 mi. S Napa	Rentschler Field	3 mi. ESE Hartford
Needles Army Airfield	5 mi. S Needles		
Oakland Municipal Airport			
(Hamilton Field, sub base)	5 mi. S Oakland	DELAWARE	
Ontario Army Air Field	1 mi. E Ontario		
Orange County Army Air Field	4 mi. S Santa Ana	Dover Army Air Field	4 mi. SE Dover
Oroville Army Air Field	3 mi. SW Oroville	New Castle Army Air Base	5 mi. SW Wilmington
Otay-Mesa NAAS	14 mi. SE San Diego		
Oxnard Flight Strip	6 mi. E. Oxnard	FLORIDA	
Palmdale Army Air Field	3 mi. NE Palmdale		
Palm Springs Army Air Field	2 mi. E Palm Springs	Alachua Army Air Field	3 mi. NE Gainesville
Parker (Gardner Field aux.)	15 mi. SE Taft	Apalachicola Army Air Field	8 mi. W Apalachicola
Potterville Army Air Field	3 mi. SW Potterville	Avon Park Army Air Field	10 mi. ENE Avon Park
Ream Field (March Field, aux.)	12 mi. S San Diego	Bartow Army Air Field	5 mi. NE Bartow
Redding Army Air Field	7 mi. SE Redding	Boca Raton Army Air Field	2 mi. NW Boca Raton
Rice Army Air Field	2 mi. ESE Rice	Brooksville Army Air Field	4 mi. S Brooksville
Sacramento Municipal Airport		Buckingham Army Air Field	4 mi. E Fort Myers
(Hamilton Field, sub base)	5 mi. S Sacramento	Bushnell Army Air Field	3 mi. NE Bushnell
Salinas Army Air Base	3 mi. SE Salinas	Carrabelle Flight Strip	2 mi. W Carrabelle
San Bernardino Army Air Depot	3 mi. ESE San Bernardino	Cross City Army Air Field	1 mi. E Cross City
San Diego Municipal Airport	1 mi. W San Diego	Dale Mabry Field	2 mi. WSW Tallahassee
San Diego Naval Air Station	North Island		

162

FIELD OR AIRSTRIP	MILES FROM NEAREST TOWN
Drew Field	5 mi. W Tampa
Dunnellon Army Air	5 mi. E Dunnellon
Eglin Field	2 mi. W Valpariso
Eglin aux. #1	14 mi. NNE Valpariso
Eglin aux. #2	6 mi. NNE Valpariso
Eglin aux. #3	10 mi. N Valpariso
Eglin aux. #4	6 mi. W Valpariso
Eglin aux. #5	10 mi. NW Valpariso
Eglin aux. #6	18 mi. WNW Valpariso
Eglin aux. #7	19 mi. W Valpariso
Eglin aux. #8	10 mi. ENE Valpariso
Eglin aux. #9	14 mi. WSW Valpariso
Hendricks Field	5 mi. SE Sebring
Hillsborough Army Air Field	6 mi. NNW Tampa
Homestead Army Air Field	5 mi. ENE Homestead
Immokalee Airfield	1 mi. NE Immokalee
Jacksonville Army Air Field	6 mi. N Jacksonville
Keystone Army Air Field	3 mi. NNW Keystone Heights
Kissimmee Army Air Field	2 mi. N Kissimmee
Lakeland Army Air Field	3 mi. N Lakeland
Lake Wales Airfield	2 mi. WSW Lake Wales
Leesburg Army Air Field	5 mi. E Leesburg
Leesburg Base Services	7 mi. NW Leesburg
Mac Dill Field	8 mi. SSW Tampa
Marathon Flight Strip	3 mi. ENE Marathon
Marianna Army Air Field	6 mi. NNE Marianna
Montbrook Army Air Field	2 mi. NW Montbrook
Morrison Field	2 mi. SW Palm Beach
Naples Army Air Field	1 mi. NE Naples
Orlando Air Base	2 mi. E Orlando
Page Field	4 mi. S Fort Myers
Palm Beach County Park	2 mi. WNW Lantana
Pan American 36th St., Army Air Base	6 mi. NW Miami
Perry Army Air Field	3 mi. S Perry
Pinecastle Army Air Field	7 mi. SE Pinecastle
Pinellas Army Air Field	10 mi. N St. Petersburg
Prospect Field (Boca Raton AAF, aux.)	1 mi. WNW Boca Raton
Punta Gorda Army Air Field	4 mi. ESE Punta Gorda
Sarasota Army Air Field	4 mi. NNW Sarasota
Taylor Field	1 mi. SW Ocala
Tyndall Field	8 mi. SE Panama City
Venice Army Air Field	Venice
Zephyrhills Army Air Field	1 mi. SE Zephyrhills

GEORGIA

FIELD OR AIRSTRIP	MILES FROM NEAREST TOWN
Adel Field	2 mi. W Adel
Atlanta Municipal Airport	8 mi. S Atlanta
Bush Field	8 mi. SSE Augusta
Bainbridge Army Air Field	4 mi. NNW Bainbridge
Bemis Field (Moody Field, aux.)	12 mi. NE Valdosta
Camp Stewart Army Air Field	3 mi. NE Hinesville
Chatham Army Air Field	6 mi. NW Savannah
Cochran Field	9 mi. S Macon
Commodore Decatur Field	2 mi. W Bainbridge
Cordele Field	2 mi. NNE Cordele
Daniel Field	3 mi. WSW Augusta
Dublin Airfield	5 mi. NW Dublin
Harris Neck Army Air Field	7 mi. ES Newport
Herbert Smart Airport	4 mi. E Macon
Homerville Flight Strip	2 mi. NW Homerville
Hunter Field	3 mi. SW Savannah
Lake Park Field (Moody Field, aux.)	12 mi. SSE Valdosta
Lawson Field	8 mi. S Columbus
Marietta Army Air Field	2 mi. SE Marietta
Moody Field	23 mi. NE Valdosta
Moultrie Field	7 mi. S Moultrie
Robins Field	17 mi. SE Macon
Spence Field	4 mi. SE Moultrie
Statesboro Army Air Field	3 mi. NE Statesboro
Sylvania Army Air Field	7 mi. SSE Sylvania
Thomasville Army Air Field	8 mi. NE Thomasville
Tifton Field	2 mi. SE Tifton
Turner Field	3 mi. E Albany
Valdosta Field	2 mi. S Valdosta
Vidalia Airfield	3 mi. SE Vidalia
Waycross Army Air Field	3 mi. NW Waycross

IDAHO

FIELD OR AIRSTRIP	MILES FROM NEAREST TOWN
Gowen Field	3 mi. S Boise
Mountain Home Army Air Base	11 mi. WSW Mountain Home
Pocatello Army Air Field	8 mi. NW Pocatello
Pocatello Field	6 mi. NW Pocatello

ILLINOIS

FIELD OR AIRSTRIP	MILES FROM NEAREST TOWN
Chanute Field	1 mi. S Rantoul
Chicago Municipal Airport	8 mi. SW Loop District
Curtiss-Steinberg	4 mi. SSW East St. Louis
George Field	4 mi. NE Lawrenceville
Orchard Place Airport	14 mi. NW Chicago
Presbyterian Church aux. #3	4 mi. WNW Lawrenceville
Scott Field	9 mi. NE Belleville
St. Charles Field	3 mi. E St. Charles

INDIANA

FIELD OR AIRSTRIP	MILES FROM NEAREST TOWN
Atterbury Army Air Field	3 mi. N Columbus
Baer Field	5 mi. SW Fort Wayne
Bendix Field	3 mi. NW South Bend
Emison (George Field, aux.)	4 mi. WSW Oaktown
Evansville Municipal Airport	5 mi. NE Evansville
Freeman Field	2 mi. S Seymour
Madison Army Air Field	5 mi. NNW Madison
St. Anne (Freeman Field, aux.)	2 mi. NNE North Vernon
Stout Field	5 mi. SW Indianapolis
Walesboro Field (Freeman Field, aux.)	1 mi. WSW Walesboro

FIELD OR AIRSTRIP	MILES FROM NEAREST TOWN	FIELD OR AIRSTRIP	MILES FROM NEAREST TOWN

IOWA

Burlington Field	2 mi. SSW Burlington
Des Moines Field	3 mi. SSW Des Moines
Sioux City Army Air Base	6 mi. SSE Sioux City

KANSAS

Atkinson Field	3 mi. NW Pittsburg
Coffeyville Army Air Field	5 mi. NNW Coffeyville
Coffeyville AAF aux. #3	16 mi. ENE Coffeyville
Coffeyville Field	2 mi. NW Coffeyville
Dodge City Army Air Field	5 mi. WNW Dodge City
Dodge City Field	3 mi. ENE Dodge City
Dodge City aux. #4	17 mi. NNE Dodge City
Fairfax Field	1 mi. N Kansas City
Garden City Army Air Field	9 mi. ESE Garden City
Garden City AAF aux. #1	19 mi. ESE Garden City
Garden City AAF aux. #2	13 mi. E Garden City
Garden City AAF aux. #3	6 mi. ENE Garden City
Great Bend Army Air Field	5 mi. W Great Bend
Herington Army Air Field	6 mi. E Herington
Independence Army Air Field	6 mi. SW Independence
Independence AAF aux. #9	12 mi. NE Independence
Liberal Army Air Field	2 mi. W Liberal
Marshall Field	2 mi. SE Fort Riley
Phillip Billard	4 mi. ENE Topeka
Pratt Army Air Field	5 mi. N Pratt
Sherman Field	1 mi. NNE Fort Leavenworth
Smoky Hill Army Air Field	5 mi. SW Salina
South Field aux. #5	4 mi. W Arkansas City
Strother Field	5 mi. SSW Winfield
Topeka Army Air Field	7 mi. S Topeka
Walker Army Air Field	1 mi. E Walker
Wichita Municipal Airport	5 mi. SE Wichita

KENTUCKY

Bowman Field	5 mi. E Louisville
Campbell Army Air Field	13 mi. NW Clarksville
Godman Field	Fort Knox
Lexington AFS	5 mi. W Lexington
Standiford Field	6 mi. SE Louisville
Paducah Municipal Airport (Nashville, aux.)	Paducah
Sturgis Army Air Field	1 mi. E Sturgis

LOUISIANA

Alexandria Army Air Field	6 mi. WNW Alexandria
Alvin Callender	8 mi. SSE New Orleans
Barksdale Field	6 mi. E Shreveport
DeRidder Army Air Base	3 mi. WSW DeRidder
Esler Field	10 mi. NE Alexandria
Hammond Army Air Field	3 mi. E Hammond
Harding Field	5 mi. N Baton Rouge

Lafayette Field	1 mi. SE Lafayette
Lake Charles Army Air Field	3 mi. ESE Lake Charles
Leesville Landing Strip	2 mi. NW Leesville
Mansfield Airfield	4 mi. NW Mansfield
Natchitoches Field	1 mi. SSW Natchitoches
New Orleans Army Air Base	6 mi. NE New Orleans
Pollock Army Air Base	4 mi. SW Pollock
Selman Field	2 mi. NW Monroe
Shreveport Field	2 mi. NNE Shreveport

MAINE

Deblois Flight Strip	2 mi. SE Deblois
Dow Field	2 mi. W Bangor
Houlton Army Air Field	2 mi. E Houlton
Pittsfield Field	1 mi. SSE Pittsfield
Presque Isle Army Air Field	2 mi. WNW Presque Isle

MARYLAND

Baltimore Army Air Field	6 mi. SE Baltimore
Edgewood Arsenal	1 mi. S Edgewood Arsenal
Fort Meade	Fort Meade
Martin Field (Baltimore AAF aux.)	10 mi. NE Baltimore
Phillips Field	5 mi. SE Aberdeen
Salisbury Airfield	1 mi. NE Salisbury
Salisbury Field #2	5 mi. ESE Salisbury

MASSACHUSETTS

Barnes Airport	3 mi. NNE Westfield
New Bedford Army Air Field	2 mi. SE Bedford
Boston Municipal Airport	4 mi. E Boston
Fort Devens Army Air Field	1 mi. NW Avers
Hyannis Airfield	1 mi. N Hyannis
New Bedford Army Air Field	2 mi. NW New Bedford
Otis Field	8 mi. NE Falmouth
Westover Field	4 mi. NE Chicopee

MICHIGAN

Alpena Army Air Field	7 mi. WNW Alpena
Detroit City Field	6 mi. NE Detroit
Grayling Army Air Field	1 mi. NW Grayling
Kalamazoo Field	4 mi. SSE Kalamazoo
Kellogg Field	3 mi. WSW Battle Creek
Kent County Field	4 mi. SSE Grand Rapids
Muskegon Field	5 mi. S Muskegon
Oscoda Army Air Field	4 mi. NW Oscoda
Romulus Army Air Field	16 mi. SW Detroit
Selfridge Field	3 mi. E Mt. Clemens
Tri-City Army Air Field	10 mi. NW Saginaw
Willow Run Airport	3 mi. E Ypsilanti

MINNESOTA

Camp Ripley Field	7 mi. N Little Falls
Flyn Field (Glider Training)	12 mi. E St. Paul
Minneapolis Field (Chamberlain)	6 mi. SSE Minneapolis
Rochester Municipal Airport	1 mi. SE Rochester
St. Paul Municipal Airport	2 mi. SE St. Paul

MISSISSIPPI

Hancock County Bombing Range	9 mi. NW Bay St. Louis
Columbus Army Air Field	10 mi. NNW Columbus
Greenville Army Air Field	8 mi. NE Greenville
Greenville-Washington County Field	2 mi. E Greenville
Greenwood Army Air Field	6 mi. SE Greenwood
Greenwood Field	2 mi. SW Greenwood
Grenada Army Air Field	4 mi. NE Grenada
Gulfport Army Air Field	3 mi. NE Gulfport
Gulfport Field	1 mi. N Gulfport
Hancock County Airport	8 mi. NW Bay St. Louis
Hinds County (Jackson AB aux.)	13 mi. W Jackson
Hattiesburg Army Air Field	4 mi. SE Hattiesburg
Jackson Air Base	3 mi. NW Jackson
Kessler Field	2 mi. W Biloxi
Key Field	3 mi. SW Meridian
Laurel Army Air Field	3 mi. SW Laurel
Lime Prairie Field (Jackson AAB aux.)	30 mi. ENE Jackson

MISSOURI

Chester Field	4 mi. NW McBride
Columbia Field	2 mi. NW Columbia
Deblois Flight Strip	2 mi. S Deblois
Dexter AAF (aux. #1)	1 mi. SSE Dexter
Fort Leonard Wood	SW corner
Gideon AAF (aux. #4)	1 mi. SE Gideon
Jefferson Barracks	10 mi. SW St. Louis
Joplin Field	5 mi. NNE Joplin
Kansas City Municipal Airport	1 mi. N Kansas City
Lambert Field	11 mi. NW St. Louis
Malden Army Air Field	2 mi. NNW Malden
Rosecrans Field	4 mi. NW St. Joseph
Sedalia Army Air Field	2 mi. S Knobnoster
Vichy Army Air Field	12 mi. W Rolla

MONTANA

Cut Bank Army Air Field	2 mi. SW Cut Bank
Dell Flight Strip	1 mi. NW Dell
Glasgow Army Air Field	3 mi. N Glasgow
Gore Field	3 mi. WSW Great Falls
Great Falls Army Air Field	4 mi. E Great Falls
Helena Field	3 mi. ENE Helena
Lewistown Army Air Field	1 mi. WSW Lewistown

NEBRASKA

Ainsworth Army Air Field	5 mi. W Ainsworth
Alliance Army Air Field	5 mi. SE Alliance
Bruning Army Air Field	8 mi. E Bruning
Fairmont Army Air Field	2 mi. S Fairmont
Grand Island Army Air Field	2 mi. NNE Grand Island
Grand Island (aux.)	2 mi. NE Grand Island
Harvard Army Air Field	2 mi. N Harvard
Kearney Army Air Field	1 mi. E Kearney
Lee Bird Field	3 mi. ESE North Platte
Lincoln Army Air Field	7 mi. NW Lincoln
McCook Army Air Field	7 mi. NNW McCook
Offutt Field	9 mi. S Omaha
Omaha Field	3 mi. NE Omaha
Scottsbluff Army Air Field	3 mi. E Scottsbluff
Scribner Army Air Field	2 mi. S Scribner
Union Field	5 mi. NNE Lincoln

NEVADA

Caliente Flight Strip	21 mi. W Caliente
Camp Raleigh Field	2 mi. S Camp Raleigh
Freeman Field	5 mi. SE Fallon
Indian Springs Army Air Field	1 mi. N Indian Springs
Lahontan Flight Strip	15 mi. S Fernley
Las Vegas Army Air Field	7 mi. NE Las Vegas
Las Vegas Airfield	6 mi. NE Las Vegas
Owyhee Flight Strip	4 mi. W Owyhee
Reno Army Air Base	10 mi. NNW Reno
Tonopah Army Air Field	8 mi. E Tonopah
Tonopah (aux. #5)	44 mi. SE Tonopah

NEW HAMPSHIRE

Claremont Field	1 mi. W Claremont
Concord Field	1 mi. ENE Concord
Grenier Field	4 mi. S Manchester
Nashua Field	3 mi. WNW Nashua
Portsmouth Airfield	3 mi. W Portsmouth

NEW JERSEY

Bendix Airport	Bendix
Caldwell-Wright Field	2 mi. N Caldwell
Fort Dix Army Air Base	1 mi. SW Wrightstown
Milleville Army Air Field	3 mi. SW Milleville
Moorestown Field	2 mi. NNE Moorestown
Newark Army Air Field	2 mi. S Newark
Fort Dix Army Air Base	1 mi. SE Wrightstown

NEW MEXICO

Field or Airstrip	Miles from Nearest Town
Alamogordo Army Air Field	9 mi. WSW Alamogordo
Albuquerque Army Air Field	3 mi. S Albuquerque
Camp Luna	7 mi. NW Las Vegas
Carlsbad Army Air Field	2 mi. S Carlsbad
Carlsbad AAF (aux. #1)	10 mi. S Carlsbad
Clovis Army Air Field	5 mi. W Clovis
Crews Field	12 mi. SSW Raton
Deming Army Air Field	2 mi. E Deming
Deming AAF (aux. #1)	19 mi. SSW Deming
Deming AAF (aux. #2)	11 mi. W Deming
Fort Sumner Army Air Field	1 mi. E Fort Sumner
Fort Sumner AAF (aux. #5)	16 mi. ENE Fort Sumner
Hobbs Army Air Field	4 mi. NW Hobbs
Kirtland Field	3 mi. SSE Albuquerque
Roswell Army Air Field	7 mi. S Roswell
Roswell AAF (aux. #1)	8 mi. SW Roswell
Santa Fe Army Air Field	10 mi. WSW Santa Fe

NEW YORK

Field or Airstrip	Miles from Nearest Town
Albany Field	7 mi. NNW Albany
Buffalo Municipal Airport	8 mi. ENE Buffalo
Elizabeth Field	West end of Fisher's Island
Farmingdale Army Air Field	1 mi. E Farmingdale
Idlewild Airfield	13 mi. SE New York
LaGuardia Field	5 mi. E New York
Mastic Flight Strip	2 mi. NW Mastic
Mitchel Field	1 mi. NE Hempstead
Montgomery Field (USMA aux. #1)	2 mi. SW Montgomery
New Hackensack (USMA aux. #3)	1 mi. W New Hackensack
Niagara Falls Field	4 mi. E Niagara Falls
Niagara Municipal Airport	6 mi. SW Niagara Falls
Rome Army Air Field	2 mi. ENE Rome
Rome Flight Strip	26 mi. S Rome
Roosevelt NAF	2 mi. ESE Mineola
Stewart Field	8 mi. NNW Newburgh
Suffolk County Army Air Field	1 mi. NE Westhampton Beach
Syracuse Field	6 mi. WNW Syracuse
Wallkill (UAMA aux. #2)	3 mi. NW Wallkill
Watertown Field	6 mi. NW Watertown
Wheeler-Sack Field	11 mi. ENE Watertown
Westchester County Airport	4 mi. NE White Plains

NORTH CAROLINA

Field or Airstrip	Miles from Nearest Town
Ashville-Hendersonville Field	12 mi. SSE Ashville
Barco Flight Strip	2 mi. W Barco
Bluethenthal Field	3 mi. NE Wilmington
Camp Davis Army Air Field	1 mi. NNE Hollyridge
Camp Mackall Field	4 mi. E Hoffman
Charlotte Municipal Field	6 mi. W Charlotte
Fairchild Aircraft Field	2 mi. E Burlington
Balloon Field (aux. #1)	1 mi. NNW Fort Bragg
Greensboro Municipal Airport	8 mi. W Greensboro
Lumberton Field #2 (Gliders)	3 mi. WSW Lumberton

Field or Airstrip	Miles from Nearest Town
Hoffman (Camp Mackall)	4 mi. NE Hoffman
Laurinburg-Maxton Army Air Base	2 mi. N Maxton
Morris Field	5 mi. WSW Charlotte
Pope Field	12 mi. NW Fayetteville
Raleigh Durham Army Air Field	11 mi. NW Raleigh Durham
Smith-Reynolds Airport	2 mi. N Winston-Salem
Seymour Johnson Field	3 mi. SE Goldsboro

NORTH DAKOTA

Field or Airstrip	Miles from Nearest Town
Bismarck Municipal Airport	2 mi. SE Bismarck
Fargo Municipal Airport	2 mi. NW Fargo

OHIO

Field or Airstrip	Miles from Nearest Town
Cleveland Municipal Airport	9 mi. SW Cleveland
Clinton County Army Air Field	1 mi. E Wilmington
Dayton Municipal Airport	12 mi. N Dayton
Lockbourne Army Air Field	9 mi. S Columbus
Lunken Airport	4 mi. E Cincinnati
Middletown Field	1 mi. N Middletown
Patterson Field	10 mi. SE Dayton
Toledo Field	7 mi. SSE Toledo
Wright Field	5 mi. E Dayton

OKLAHOMA

Field or Airstrip	Miles from Nearest Town
Altus Army Air Field	2 mi. ENE Altus
Ardmore Army Air Field	9 mi. N Ardmore
Bethany Field #2	8 mi. WNW Oklahoma City
Enid Army Air Field	5 mi. SSW Enid
Frederick Army Air Field	2 mi. SE Frederick
Gage Airfield (Will Rogers Field aux.)	2 mi. SSW Gage
Great Salt Plains Bombing Range	5 mi. NE Jet
Hobart Airfield	3 mi. SE Hobart
Miami Field	2 mi. NNW Miami
Muskogee Airport	2 mi. W Muskogee
Muskogee Army Air Field (Will Rogers Field S.B.)	5 mi. S Muskogee
Perry Airfield	6 mi. N Perry
Ponca City Field	3 mi. NNW Ponca City
Tinker Field	9 mi. SE Oklahoma City
Tulsa Field	6 mi. NE Tulsa
Tulsa AAF	7 mi. ENE Tulsa
Will Rogers Field	7 mi. SW Oklahoma City
Woodring Field	5 mi. ESE Enid
Woodward Army Air Field	7 mi. W Woodward

OREGON

Field or Airstrip	Miles from Nearest Town
Alkali Lake Flight Strip	14 mi. SW Wagontire
Aurora Flight Strip	1 mi. NW Aurora
Boardman Flight Strip	5 mi. WSW Boardman
Corvallis Army Air Field	2 mi. S Corvallis

Field or Airstrip	Miles from Nearest Town
Eugene Municipal Airport	7 mi. NW Eugene
Hillsboro Municipal Airport	2 mi. NE Hillsboro
Madris Army Air Field	2 mi. NNW Madris
Mahlon Sweet Field	8 mi. NW Eugene
McMinnville Airfield	3 mi. ESE McMinnville
Medford Army Air Field	2 mi. N Medford
Pendleton Field	3 mi. NW Pendleton
Portland Army Air Base	6 mi. NNE Portland
Redmond Army Air Field	1 mi. ESE Redmond
Rome Flight Strip	27 mi. SW Rome
Salem Army Air Field	1 mi. SE Salem
The Dalles Field	2 mi. NE The Dalles

PENNSYLVANIA

Field or Airstrip	Miles from Nearest Town
Connellsville Municipal Airport	5 mi. SW Connellsville
Harrisburg Municipal Airport	4 mi. S Harrisburg
Olmstead Field	1 mi. W Middletown
Philadelphia Municipal Airport	6 mi. SW Philadelphia
Pittsburg-Allegheny County Airport	7 mi. SE Pittsburgh
Reading Army Air Field	3 mi. NW Reading
Waynesboro Municipal Airport	3 mi. SE Waynesboro
Williamsport Field	4 mi. E Williamsport

RHODE ISLAND

Field or Airstrip	Miles from Nearest Town
Hillsgrove Army Air Field	5 mi. S Providence

SOUTH CAROLINA

Field or Airstrip	Miles from Nearest Town
Aiken Army Air Field	7 mi. NNE Aiken
Anderson Airfield (Greenville AAB aux.)	3 mi. W Anderson
Barnwell Airfield (Columbia AAB aux.)	2 mi. NW Barnwell
Charlestown Army Air Field	10 mi. NW Charlestown
Chester Airfield	6 mi. NNE Chester
Columbia Army Air Base	6 mi. SW Columbia
Congaree Army Air Field	15 mi. ESE Columbia
Coranca Army Air Field	4 mi. N Greenwood
Florence Army Air Field	2 mi. ESE Florence
Greenville Army Air Base	7 mi. SSE Greenville
Greenville Municipal Airport	3 mi. E Greenville
Hartsfield Airfield (Greenville AAB aux.)	3 mi. N Hartsfield
Johns Island Airfield (Columbia AAB aux.)	7 mi. SSW Charlestown
Myrtle Beach Army Air Field	3 mi. WSW Myrtle Beach
North Airfield	1 mi. ESE North
Ocean Drive Flight Strip	3 mi. WSW Ocean Drive
Owens Field	3 mi. SE Columbia
Shaw Field	7 mi. NW Sumter
Spartanburg Airfield	2 mi. SSW Spartanburg
Walterboro Army Air Field	2 mi. NE Walterboro
Wampee Flight Strip	3 mi. S Wampee

SOUTH DAKOTA

Field or Airstrip	Miles from Nearest Town
Mitchell Army Air Field	4 mi. N Mitchell
Pierre Army Air Field	4 mi. ENE Pierre
Rapid City Army Air Base	9 mi. NE Rapid City
Sioux Falls Army Air Field	3 mi. NE Sioux Falls
Watertown Army Air Field	2 mi. NW Watertown

TENNESSEE

Field or Airstrip	Miles from Nearest Town
Berry Field	6 mi. SE Nashville
Dyersburg Army Air Field	12 mi. S Dyersburg
McKeller Field	5 mi. W Jackson
Memphis Municipal Airport	8 mi. SE Memphis
Smyrna Army Air Field	1 mi. N Smyrna
Tri-City Field	12 mi. NNW Tri-City
Wm. Nothern Field	2 mi. NW Tullahoma

TEXAS

Field or Airstrip	Miles from Nearest Town
Abernathy Field	6 mi. E Abernathy
Abilene Air Terminal	3 mi. ESE Abilene
Abilene Army Air Field	7 mi. WSW Abilene
Alamo Field	7 mi. NNE San Antonio
Aloe Army Air Field	4 mi. WSW Victoria
Aloe AAF (aux. #10)	20 mi. WSW Victoria
Amarillo Army Air Field	9 mi. ENE Amarillo
Amarillo Field	6 mi. ENE Amarillo
Avenger Field	4 mi. W Sweetwater
Bergstrom Field	8 mi. E Austin
Biggs Field	8 mi. NE El Paso
Big Spring Army Air Field	3 mi. W Big Spring
Big Spring Army Glider School	18 mi. NNW Big Spring
Biggs Field	6 mi. NE El Paso
Blackland Army Air Field	3 mi. W Big Spring
Brooks Field	3 mi. SSE San Antonio
Brownsville Municipal Airport	5 mi. E Brownsville
Brownwood Army Air Field	5 mi. NNE Brownwood
Bryan Army Air Field	5 mi. SW Bryan
Childress Army Air Field	3 mi. W Childress
Cox Field	5 mi. ESE Paris
Dalhart Army Air Field	3 mi. SSW Dalhart
Dalhart Sub Base #1	10 mi. W Dalhart
Dalhart Sub Base #2	11 mi. NE Dalhart
Dyche Field	9 mi. SW Fort Stockton
Eagle Pass Army Air Field	10 mi. NE Eagle Pass
Ellington Field	12 mi. SE Houston
Ellington aux. #2	3 mi. WNW Houston
El Paso Municipal Airport	5 mi. ENE El Paso
Fort Worth Army Air Field	7 mi. WNW Fort Worth
Foster Field	5 mi. NE Victoria
Foster aux. #4	13 mi. NNW Victoria
Gainsville Army Air Field	3 mi. WNW Gainsville
Galveston Army Air Field	5 mi. SW Galveston
Gaskin Field (Perrin Field aux.)	13 mi. SW Sherman
Gibbs Field	2 mi. NNW Fort Stockton
Goodfellow Field	3 mi. SE San Angelo
Harlingen Army Air Field	3 mi. NE Harlingen

167

Hensley Field	11 mi. NW Dallas	**VIRGINIA**	
Hondo Army Air Field	1 mi. W Hondo		
Houston Field	9 mi. SSE Houston	Blackstone Army Air Field	2 mi. ESE Blackstone
Idalou (aux. #2)	5 mi. ENE Idalou	Langley Field	3 mi. W Hampton
Kelly Field	5 mi. SW San Antonio	Melfa Flight Strip	1 mi. SW Melfa
Kelly Field (aux. #4)	5 mi. N Castroville	Norfolk Army Air Field	5 mi. NE Norfolk
Laguna Madre (Sub		Petersburg Field	6 mi. WSW Petersburg
Base-Harlingen)	Harlingen	Richmond Army Air Base	6 mi. SE Richmond
Lamesa Field	8 mi. N Lamesa	Tappahannock Flight Strip	1 mi. SW Tappahannock
Laredo Army Air Field	1 mi. NE Laredo	West Point Field	2 mi. ESE West Point
Laredo aux.	60 mi. NW Laredo	Woordum	4 mi. NNW Roanoke
Laughlin Field	6 mi. E Del Rio		
Louis Schreiner Field	4 mi. SE Kerrville		
Love Field	6 mi. N Dallas	**WASHINGTON**	
Lubbock Army Air Field	10 mi. SW Lubbock		
Majors Field	5 mi. SSW Greenville	Arlington NAAS	3 mi. SW Arlington
Majors (aux. #1)	11 mi. SW Greenville	Bellingham Army Air Field	3 mi. NW Bellingham
Majors (aux. #3)	10 mi. NNE Greenville	Boeing Field	5 mi. S Seattle
Marfa Army Air Field	8 mi. ESE Marfa	Ellensburg Army Air Field	2 mi. N Ellensburg
Marfa Field	4 mi. N Marfa	Ephrata Army Air Base	1 mi. SE Ephrata
Matagorda Island Bomb Range	8 mi. SW Port O'Connor	Felts Field	5 mi. NE Spokane
Midland Army Air Field	8 mi. WSW Midland	Fort George Wright	5 mi. NW Spokane
Midland Municipal Airport	3 mi. NNW Midland	Geiger Field	6 mi. SW Spokane
Mineral Wells Field	3 mi. SE Mineral Wells	Gray Field	1 mi. SE Fort Lewis
Moore Field	12 mi. NNW Mission	Kitsap County Airport	8 mi. SW Bremerton
Moore aux. #1	10 mi. N Edinburg	McChord Field	9 mi. S Tacoma
Moore aux. #3	4 mi. N La Grulla	Moses Lake Army Air Field	6 mi. NW Moses Lake
Palestine Field	5 mi. WNW Palestine	Mt. Vernon Navy Airport	6 mi. NW Mt. Vernon
Palacios Army Air Field	3 mi. NW Palacios	Olympia Army Air Field	4 mi. S Olympia
Pampa Army Air Field	12 mi. E Pampa	Omak Flight Strip	Omak
Pecos Army Air Field	2 mi. S Pecos	Paine Field	5 mi. SW Everett
Perrin Field	6 mi. NW Sherman	Port Angeles Army Air Field	3 mi. W Port Angeles
Pounds Field	6 mi. W Tyler	Quillayute Navy Airport	1 mi. SW Quillayute
Pyote Field	1 mi. SW Pyote	Shelton Navy Airport	2 mi. NW Shelton
Randolph Field	17 mi. NE San Antonio	South Bend Airfield	6 mi. WNW Willapa
San Angelo Army Air Field	8 mi. SSW San Angelo	Spokane Army Air Field	10 mi. WSW Spokane
San Antonio Field	7 mi. N San Antonio	Walla Walla Army Air Field	2 mi. NE Walla Walla
San Marcos Army Air Field	3 mi. E San Marcos	Yakima Airfield	Yakima
Sheppard Field	6 mi. N Wichita Falls		
Sherman Field	1 mi. NE Fort		
	Leavenworth	**WISCONSIN**	
South Plains Army Air Field	5 mi. N Lubbock		
Stinson Field	6 mi. S San Antonio	Billy Mitchell Field	3 mi. W Lake Michigan
Temple Army Air Field	6 mi. NW Temple	Camp Williams Army Air Field	1 mi. N Camp Douglas
Terrell Field	2 mi. SSE Terrell	Camp McCoy	3 mi. E Camp McCoy
Waco Army Air Field	5 mi. NE Waco	Tomah	15 mi. E Sparta
Waco Field	3 mi. W Waco	Truax Field	3 mi. NE Madison
Wink Field	4 mi. NW Wink		
		WYOMING	
UTAH			
		Casper Army Air Field	6 mi. NNW Casper
Dugway Field	45 mi. SW Tooele	Cheyenne Municipal Airport	2 mi. N Cheyenne
Hill Field	9 mi. SW Ogden		
Hinckley Field	5 mi. W Ogden	**WASHINGTON, D.C.**	
Logan-Cache County Field	4 mi. NNW Logan		
Low Flight Strip	3 mi. N Knolls	Bolling Field	3 mi. S D.C.
Salt Lake City Army Air Base	4 mi. W Salt Lake City	Camp Springs Army Air Field	11 mi. SE D.C.
Salt Lake Field #2	11 mi. SW Salt Lake City	Washington National Airport	3 mi. S D.C.
Wendover Field	1 mi. S Wendover		

References

CHAPTER 1

Forgotten Fields of America, Lou Thole: Pictorial Histories Publishing Co. Inc., Missoula, Montana, 1996.
Dissecting an Air Force, Russell Lee: AAHS Journal, American Aviation Historical Society, Santa Ana, California, Spring 1999.

CHAPTER 2

A Pictorial History of Nellis Air Force Base, 1941–1946, J. Catherene Wilman PH.D., and Senior Airman James Reinhardt: Office of History, Headquarters Air Warfare Center, Nellis AFB, Nevada, 1997.
Benjamin O. Davis, Jr.—American, Benjamin O. Davis, Jr.: Smithsonian Institution Press, Washington, D.C., and London, 1991.
Blacks in The Army Air Forces During World War II, Alan Osur: Office of Air Force History, Washington, D.C., 1997.
History of the 66th AAF Flying Training Detachment, Moton Field, Tuskegee Institute, Alabama, 1st Lieutenant Joseph Hensley: Air Force History Support Office, Bolling AFB, Washington, D.C.
Lonely Eagles, Robert Rose D.D.S.: Tuskegee Airman Inc., Los Angeles Chapter, Los Angeles, California, 1976.
Mister: The Training of an Aviation Cadet in World War II, Eugene Fletcher: University of Washington Press, 1992.
Negroes and the Air Force, 1939–1949, Lawrence Paszek: USAAF Historical Division, Historical Studies Branch.
Segregated Skies: All Black Combat Squadrons of World War II, Stanley Sandler: Smithsonian Institution Press, Washington, D.C., and London, 1992.
The Tuskegee Airman, Charles Francis: Bruce Humphries, Inc. Boston, Mass., 1955.
Tuskegee Airman, Moton Field/Tuskegee Airman, Special Resource Study, National Park Service, Atlanta, Georgia, 1997.
WASHOUT! Charles Watry: California Aero Press, Carlsbad, 1983.
Moton Field/Tuskegee Airmen, Special Resource Study, United States Department of the Interior,

National Park Service Atlanta, Georgia 1998.
Conversations/Correspondence: Col. R.J. Lewis, USAF (Ret), Dr. Daniel Williams, Mr. John Leahr, Mr. Ed (Don) Doram, Mr. Godfrey Miller, Mr. Bill Childs, Mr. Gene Carter, Mr. Hank Sanford, Mr. Charles (Briggie) Brown, Mr. Wardell Polk, Ms. Christine Trebellas, and Dr. Robert Schultz.

CHAPTER 3

DeSoto County Times, various articles.
Sun Herald, article 10/30/94.
Cadets Handbook, Riddle Aeronautical Institute, Carlstrom Field, Arcadia, Florida; 1943.
The Army Air Forces in World War II. Vol. VI, Craven & Cate: The University of Chicago Press, Chicago, Illinois, 1955.
A Bit of Britain in Arcadia's Oak Ridge Cemetery: Read Harding.
British Aircrew Training in the United States, 1941–1945, Gilbert Guinn: Air Power History, Summer, 1995.
Carlstrom Field, Army and Navy Publishing Co., Inc., Baton Rouge, Louisiana, 1942.
Correspondence/conversations: Colonel and Mrs. George Ola, USAF (Ret.)

CHAPTER 4

Station History—Buckingham Army Air Field, USAF Historical Research Center, Maxwell AFB, Alabama.
Directory of Airfields (Continental United States), commanding General Army Air Forces. AC/AS Operations and Requirements, Requirements Division, Aeronautical Chart Service, Washington, D.C., 2/1/1944.
Fort Myers News Press, Fort Myers, Florida, 10/22/89, 5/12/85.
The Miami Herald, Miami, Florida, 6/13/60.
Flexigun (the base newspaper), Buckingham Field Army Air Forces Flexible Gunnery School, Fort Myers, Florida.
The Making of An Aerial Gunner, Robert Serveiss, Friends Journal, Air Force Museum Foundation, Inc., Winter 1991.
Aerial Gunners The Unknown Aces of World War

II, Charles Waltry and Duane Hall, California Aero Press, Carlsbad, California, 1986.

Operation Pinball, Ivan Hickman, Motorbooks International, Osceola, Wisconsin, 1990.

U.S. Army Aircraft, 1908–1946, James C. Fahey, Ship and Aircraft, Falls Church, Virginia, 1946.

Jane's Fighting Aircraft Of World War II, Military Press, Crown Publishers, Inc, New York, NY, 1989.

Various data and material from the collection of Mr. Jimmy Porter, Buckingham, Florida.

Air Power History, Air Force Historical Foundation, Washington D. C., Vol. 42, Number 4, Winter 1995.

Correspondence/conversations: Mr. Jimmy Porter, Mr. Jim Green, Mr. Buddy Frazier, Mr. Leroy Knorr, and Mr. Ernie Hix.

CHAPTER 5

Station History, San Angelo AAF, USAF Historical Research Agency, Maxwell Air Force Base, Alabama.

The Young Men Behind Plexiglass, _____

The Army Air Forces in World War II, Men and Planes, vol. VI; Craven and Cate, The University of Chicago Press, Chicago, ILL, 1955

The Home Front: U.S.A., Ronald H. Bailey, Time Life Books Inc., Alexandria VA, 1978.

U.S. Army Aircraft—1908–1945, James C. Fahey, Ships and Aircraft, Falls Church, VA, 1946.

San Angelo Standard Times, San Angelo, Texas, 1942—various articles.

History of Air Training Command 1943–1993, Thomas Manning, Office of History and Research, Headquarters, Air Education and Training Command, Randolph AFB, TX, 1993.

Correspondence/conversations: Dr. Edwin Sykes, Mr. Louis Drake, Mr. Warren Hasse, Mr. Roger Myers, Mr. Kent Elliot, Mr. Ross McSwain, Mr. C. M. Kahl, Ms. Suzanne Campbell.

CHAPTER 6

Station History, Hondo Army Air Field, U.S.A.F. Historical research Center, Maxwell AFB, Alabama.

Hondo Anvil Herald, Hondo Texas, various articles.

History of Air Training Command, 1943–1993, Thomas Manning, Office of History and Research Headquarters, Air Education and Training Command, Randolph Air Force Base, Texas, 1993.

With Courage—The U.S. Army Air Forces in World War II, Alfred Beck, Chief Editor, Air Force History & Museums Program, Washington, D.C. 1994.

The Army Air Forces in World War II, Wesley Craven and James Cate, the University of Chicago Press, 1955.

We'll Find the Way, Robert D Thompson, Eakin Press, Austin, Texas, 1992.

Correspondence / conversations: Dr. Robert Schultz, Mr. William Berger, Mr. Elmo Pope, Mr. Jack Taylor, Mr. Bill Ney, Mr. Otis Burrell, and Ms. Evelyn Herrmann.

CHAPTER 7

Brief History of Wendover Air Force Base—1940–1956, USAF Historical Division, Research Studies Institute, Maxwell AFB, Alabama, July 1956.

World's Largest Military Reserve: Wendover Air Force Base, 1941–63, Leonard Arrington and Thomas Alexander, Utah Historical Quarterly, Vol. 31, No 4, Fall 1963.

A Brief History of Wendover Airport, Barbara Johnson, FAA, December 1990.

History of Wendover Air Force Base, Part II, Temporary Buildings, U. S. Air Force Legal Office, Hill Air Force Base, Ogden, Utah.

Project W-47, James Rowe, Ja A Ro Publishing, Livermore, California, 1978.

Station History, Wendover Air Force Base, USAF Historical Research Center, Maxwell AFB, Alabama.

Correspondence/conversations: Mr. Chris Melville, Dr. Donald Klinko.

CHAPTER 8

Station History, Walnut Ridge Army Air Field, USAF Historical Research Center, Maxwell AFB, Alabama.

A Brief Concerning the History of the Walnut Ridge Army Airfield, Bill Hackworth: The Lawrence County Historical Quarterly, Vol. 8, Fall 1985.

The Times Dispatch, Walnut Ridge, Arkansas, various articles.

Pocahontas Star Herald, Pocahontas, Arkansas, article.

Military Surplus Airplanes, Vol. 1, 1995, General Aviation Series, Challenge Publications, Inc., Canoga Park, California.

The Martin B-26 Marauder, J.K.Havener: Southern Heritage Press, St. Petersburg, Florida, 1998.

Conversations/Correspondence: Mr. Bill Flippo, Mr. Howard Harrett, Harlon and Glenda Jones, Judge Harry Ponder, Mrs. Roberta Williams, and Dr. H. E. Williams (deceased).

CHAPTER 9

Station History—Pyote Army Air Field, USAF Historical Research Center, Maxwell AFB, Alabama.

History of Pyote Army Air Field (16th Bombardment

Operational Training Wing), July–September 1945, Air Force History Support Office, Bolling Air Force Base, Washington, D.C.

Air Force Combat Units of World War II, Mauer—Mauer: Office of Air Force History, Washington, D.C., 1983.

Epitaph for an Air Field, Periodical, Vol. V. No. 3, Fall 1973, Herb Hart: Council on Abandoned Military Posts, U.S.A., Inc., Fort Belvoir, Virginia.

The Rattlesnake Bomber Base of Texas, Periodical, Jim Marks: Council on Abandoned Military Posts, U.S.A., Inc., Fort Belvoir, Virginia.

The Rattler, base newspaper, Pyote AAF, Pyote Texas.

The Monahans News, Monahans Texas, April 20, 1987.

The Rattlesnake Bomber Base Museum Dedication Ceremony Booklet, Monahans Chamber of Commerce, April 22, 1978.

The Army Air Forces in World War II, Vol. VI, Wesley Craven and James Cate: The University of Chicago Press, Chicago Illinois, 1955.

Saga of the Superfortress, Steve Birdsall: Doubleday & Company, Inc., Garden City, N.Y. 1980.

Air Combat Special, The Boeing B-17G, Robert Jarvis, and Mary Freudenberger: Eagle Aviation Enterprises, Rockaway, N.J., 1971.

Correspondence/Conversations, Col. Jim Marks, U.S.A.F. (Ret.), Mr. Jim Carr, Maj. Gen. Joseph Dickman, U.S.A.F.(Ret.), Major P.J. Mc Laughlin, U.S.A.F. (Ret.), Col. John Carah, U.S.A.F. (Ret.), Mr. John Copeland, Mr. Bill Switzer, Mr. Dave Bellmore.

CHAPTER 10

B-29 Superfortress, Pratt Army Air Base: Quenten Hannawald, Pratt, Kansas.

Brief History of Pratt Army Air Field, 1943–1945, USAF Historical Research Division, Maxwell AFG, Alabama, 1958.

The Superfortress Is Born, Thomas Collison: Duell, Sloan, & Pearce, New York, N.Y., 1945.

B-29 Superfortress, Chester Marshall: Motorbooks International, Osceola, Wisconsen, 1993.

Pratt Daily Tribune, Pratt Kansas, various articles, 1945–1947

The Pratt Tailwind, base newspaper, Pratt Army Airfield, Kansas.

Saga of the Superfortress, Steve Birdsall: Doubleday & Company, Inc., Garden City, N.Y. 1980

Air Force Combat Units of World War Two, Mauer Mauer: Office of Air Force History, Washington, D.C., 1983.

Pratt Army Air Base, 1943–1945; Fiftieth Year Souvenir: Dorotha Giannangelo, Pratt County Historical Society, 1995.

Pratt Union, Pratt Kansas; article 5-18-'44.

Correspondence/conversations: Mr. Quenten Hannawald, Ms. Dorotha Giannangelo.

CHAPTER 11

1942—The First Year, Earl Belt: Sioux City, Iowa, 1989.

1943—The Second Year, Earl Belt: Sioux City, Iowa, 1989.

1944—The Third Year, Earl Belt: Sioux City, Iowa, 1989.

1945—The Final Year, Earl Belt: Sioux City, Iowa, 1989.

Sioux City and the Military—1941–1945: Earl Belt, Sioux City, Iowa, 1989.

The Wahkaw, Vol. VIII, #4, Summer 1989, and Vol. IX, #1, Fall 1989, the Woodbury County Genealogical Society, Sioux City, 1989.

Air Force Combat Units of World War II, Mauer Mauer: Office of Air Force History, Washington, D.C., 1983.

Airplane Accidents in the Continental US, Air Force History Support Office, Bolling Air Force Base, Washington, D.C.

Correspondence/conversations: Mr. Earl Belt, Mr. Terry Turner, Col Dennis Swanstrom, Mr. Melvin Scott, Mr. Ted Gondeck, Mr. Bob Stolze, Ms. Linda Kuester, Mr. Floyd Clark, Mr. Warren Nelson.

CHAPTER 12

Craig Air Force Base: Its Effect on Selma, 1940–1977, Carl Morgan Jr.: The Alabama Review, April 1989.

History of Craig Field: USAF Historical research Agency, Maxwell AFB, Alabama.

Bruce Kilpatrick Craig, Craig Air Force Base, Historical Division: Homer Hyde, 1953.

The Selma Times-Journal, various articles.

Craig Air Force Base Fact Sheet, Office of Information, Craig AFB, Alabama, circa 1972.

The Army Air Forces in World War II, Craven & Cate, The University of Chicago Press, Chicago, Illinois, 1955.

History of Air Training Command, 1943–1993, Thomas Mannig: Office of History and Research Headquarters, Randolph Air Force Base, Texas, 1993.

The Martin B-26 Marauder, J.K. Havner: Southern Heritage Press, St. Petersburg, Florida, 1998.

Conversations/correspondence: Mr. George Swift, Mr. Reuben Bishop, Mr. Otha Carneal, Mr. Charles Himes, Mr. Earl Siddens, Ms. Pat Hughen, Ms. Jean Martin.

About the Author

Lou Thole has written many aviation articles, most of which focus on World War II, USAAF training fields. He is a noted aviation historian, whose work has been published in newspapers and magazines including the *Friends Journal* (the publication of the Air Force Museum) and *FlyPast*. A retired sales manager, he holds a private pilot license and a glider rating. Lou lives in Cincinnati, Ohio, with his wife, Jane. They are the parents of three children.